A Travel ✦ Guide to
COLONIAL NEW YORK

By James Barter

LUCENT BOOKS®

GALE

San Diego • Detroit • New York • San Francisco • Cleveland • New Haven, Conn. • Waterville, Maine • London • Munich

On cover: The Tontine Coffee House and surrounding neighborhood,
at the corner of Wall and Water Streets.

LIBRARY OF CONGRESS CATALOGING-IN-PUBLICATION DATA

Barter, James, 1946–
    Colonial New York / by James Barter.
        p. cm. — (A travel guide to)
Summary: A visitor's guide to the weather, transportation, overnight accommodations,
dining, shopping, sightseeing, and entertainment of New York City in colonial times.
Includes bibliographical references and index.
    ISBN 1-59018-250-2 (hardcover : alk. paper)
    1. New York (N.Y.)—History—Colonial period, ca. 1600–1775—Juvenile literature.
2. New York (N.Y.)—Social life and customs—To 1775—Juvenile literature. 3. New York
(N.Y.)—Guidebooks—Juvenile literature. [1. New York (N.Y.)—History—Colonial period,
ca. 1600–1775. 2. New York (N.Y.)—Social life and customs—To 1775.] I. Title. II. Travel
guide (Lucent Books)
    F128.4.B28 2004
    974.7'102—dc22

                                                                                    2003013852

Printed in the United States of America

Contents

Travel can be a unique way to learn about oneself and other cultures. The esteemed American writer and historian, John Hope Franklin, poetically expressed his conviction in the value of travel by urging, "We must go beyond textbooks, go out into the bypaths and untrodden depths of the wilderness and travel and explore and tell the world the glories of our journey." The message communicated by this eloquent entreaty is clear: The value of travel is to temper one's imagination about a place and its people with reality, and instead of thinking how things may be, to be able to experience them as they really are.

Franklin's voice is not alone in his summons for students to "travel and explore." He is joined by a stentorian chorus of thinkers that includes former president John F. Kennedy, who established the Peace Corps to facilitate cross-cultural understandings between Americans and citizens of other lands. Ideas about the benefits of travel do not spring only from contemporary times. The ancient Greek historian Herodotus journeyed to foreign lands for the purpose of immersing himself in unfa-

miliar cultural traditions. In this way, he believed, he might gain a first-hand understanding of people and ways of life in other places.

The joys, insights, and satisfaction that travelers derive from their journeys are not limited to cultural understanding. Travel has the added value of enhancing the traveler's inner self by expanding his or her range of experiences. Writer Paul Tournier concurs that, "The real meaning of travel, like that of a conversation by the fireside, is the discovery of oneself through contact with other people."

The Lucent Books Travel Guide series enlivens history by introducing a new and innovative style and format. Each volume in the series presents the history of a preeminent historical travel destination written in the casual style and format of a travel guide. Whether providing a tour of fifth-century B.C. Athens, Renaissance Florence, or Shakespeare's London, each book describes a city or area at its cultural peak and orients readers to only those places and activities that are known to have existed at that time.

A high level of authenticity is achieved in the Travel Guide series. Each book is written in the present tense and addresses the reader as a prospective foreign traveler. The sense of authenticity is further achieved, whenever possible, by the inclusion of descriptive quotations by contemporary writers who knew the place; information on fascinating historical sites; and travel tips meant to explain unusual cultural idiosyncrasies that give depth and texture to all great cultural centers. Even shopping details, such as where to buy an ermine-trimmed gown, or a much-needed house slave, are included to inform readers of what items were sought after throughout history.

Looked at collectively, this series presents an appealing presentation of many of the cultural and social highlights of Western civilization. The collection also provides a framework for discussion about the larger historical currents that dominated not only each travel destination but countries and entire continents as well. Each book is customized by the author to bring to the fore the most important and most interesting characteristics that define each title. High standards of scholarship are assured in the series by the generous peppering of relevant quotes and extensive bibliographies. These tools provide readers a scholastic standard for their own research as well as a guide to direct them to other books, periodicals, and websites that will provide them greater breadth and detail.

America's Finest City

New York is just now beginning to emerge from the shambles of the War of Independence against England. Like any city that has been occupied by an enemy during a long and arduous conflict, New York suffered terribly from the chaos of invading soldiers, cannon fire, and general neglect of basic maintenance on roads, wharves, and municipal buildings. Following eight years of bloody strife that ended in 1783, the past ten years have been a busy period for New Yorkers rebuilding, renovating, cleaning, and expanding this unique city. Now, in 1793, New York City planners remain hard at work to eliminate the last remaining scars of war and the few remaining symbols of the English Crown.

Until recently most streets remained rutted and filthy, the docks were lit-

Hoisting the Stars and Stripes

tered with the charred hulks of burned-out ships, churches that the English had converted into stables for their cavalry smelled of horses, stylish shops were boarded up to prevent looting, and the refuse of war was strewn throughout the city's common areas and public parks.

Individual families have suffered as well. Families forced to escape the city's turmoil returned to their homes after several years to find them badly in need of repair. During the war that began in 1775, British soldiers commandeered local homes for use as their quarters with little regard for proper care. In many cases, they either carried away family furniture for barricades or burned it during the winters to keep warm. When the soldiers finally abandoned the city on November 25, 1783, a day all New Yorkers

The corner of Wall and Water streets buzzes with activity. This busy block is one of many interesting and colorful New York City neighborhoods.

celebrate as Evacuation Day, the departing English soldiers intentionally broke windows, smashed doors, and in some cases set fire to the houses.

Today, New York is emerging from the end of this dark yet historically significant period. The city is surging forward to lay claim to the unofficial title of "America's Finest City" in a competition with Boston and Philadelphia. New York's future is beginning to brighten as robust trade with Europe resumes to levels that far exceed the prewar period. Financial and commercial companies are also greatly encouraged by an expanding world of opportunity to trade

with China, South America, and the West Indies.

Exotic international trade has financially enriched the lives of many families who have the money to demand the same high quality of life found in London, Amsterdam, and Paris. The one ingredient missing before and during the war was a rich variety of cultural offerings. At last, New York is able to offer unrivaled opportunities in the fine arts and drama in theaters, music halls, and museums.

This year, New Yorkers are celebrating the city's reemergence. Plans are under way to commemorate the tenth anniversary of the two most significant days in

The stately architecture of Federal Hall makes it one of New York's most handsome historical landmarks. The city is full of cultural and architectural treasures like these.

the city's history: Evacuation Day and the signing of the Declaration of Independence. Although the Declaration of Independence was signed seventeen years ago on July 4, 1776, New York citizens were prevented from holding public annual celebrations until the war ended in 1783.

If you cannot visit New York for the Fourth of July festivities, perhaps you can join in the Evacuation Day festivities. Whichever commemoration you might choose to attend, New Yorkers have been hard at work rebuilding, renovating, expanding, painting, and beautifying the city for guests. First-time visitors will find cultural opportunities, renovated historical monuments, casual entertainment, and shops filled with tempting gifts. Once first-time visitors give the city a try, they begin to understand why New Yorkers could not possibly consider living anywhere else.

Seal of the State of New York

Chapter 1

A Brief History

Old-timers talk about a variety of Indian tribes that inhabited the New York area for as far back as anyone can tell. Long before the Americans and the English, tribes like the Munsee, Unami, Esopu, and Minsi inhabited New York. All were members of the greater Lenape Indian Nation. The name Lenape means "original people," and when anyone asks them where they came from, they always answer that they sprang from the soil. Their history goes back so many centuries that they cannot remember or conceive of a time when they did not live here.

A tribal mark of the greater Lenape Indian Nation

Visitors are not likely to encounter any Indians in New York, or for that matter anywhere in the surrounding area. Most of the land was purchased from the Indians and some was taken from them as they were driven west by the expansion of European colonists. Nonetheless, for more than a thousand years, Indian tribes living in the greater New York region planted the soil, hunted the forests, and fished the coastal waters. Women raised corn, beans, squash, and sunflowers, collected shellfish and wild foods, and made clothing from deer hides, painting them with intricate designs depicting plants and animals. Indian men hunted deer, moose, and smaller animals with bows and arrows and fished from riverbanks and dugout canoes using nets, hooks, and traps.

Lenape tribes lived near the shore in the summer months to take advantage of the fishing but moved inland during winter when the bitter north winds began to blow. Seeking protection from the piercing winds, they took shelter in

Before the Europeans arrived, the Lenape's unusually shaped longhouses were found on Manhattan Island. Today, visitors to New York will probably not meet any native people.

their dome-shaped wigwams and long-houses made of saplings and branches covered with bark, deerskins, and woven mats. Inside, Indian families kept warm by open fires, slept on mats and furs, and cooked using pottery bowls, wooden spoons, and seashells.

Beginning in the late fifteenth century, native people sporadically encountered European traders hoping to exchange their metal tools, cloth, and other foreign goods for Indian furs and agricultural surpluses. In particular, part of this trade also focused on wampum—small beads made of white or purple seashells sewed to strips of leather which served as ornaments and a form of money recognized by all tribes on the Atlantic coast. Beads were strung together in short lengths of about one foot or in much longer ones up to six feet.

Indians in the New York area grew corn, beans, squash, and other crops.

The Coming of the Europeans

The relatively simple and bucolic existence of the Lenape was not destined to last forever. In 1524 Giovanni da Verrazano, an Italian explorer flying the flag of France, inadvertently sailed his ship, *La Dauphine*, up an uncharted narrow inlet from the Atlantic Ocean to Upper New York Bay, at the southern tip of Manhattan Island. Verrazano

11

provided this earliest literary description of Manhattan and the Indians that greeted him:

The people are . . . clad with feathers of fowls of diverse colors. They came toward us very cheerfully, making great shouts of admiration, showing us where we might come to land most safely with our boat. We entered up the said river into the land about half a league, where it made a most pleasant lake [Upper New York Bay] about 3 leagues [9 miles] in compass [diameter]; on the which they rowed from the one side to the other, to the number of 30 in their small boats, wherein were many people, which passed from

The Meaning of Wampum

Wampum, called *sewant* by the Dutch, was simplistically viewed as an interesting and amusing form of Indian money by the Europeans. To them, seashells, strings of colorful glass beads, polished pebbles, and other trinkets were nothing more than simple and childish goods to be traded for the more valuable beaver furs that could be sold for enormous profits to coat and hatmakers in Europe.

To the Indians, however, wampum was much more complex. Wampum had been a sacred commodity long before the European traders arrived, and it also had a spiritual component that came from its mythological origins. In the belief systems of many northeastern Indians, wampum was delivered through powerful spirits that were tribal gods. Equally important to the understanding of wampum is the Indian belief that the exchange of these gifts could assure long life, physical and spiritual well-being, and success in undertakings such as hunting, fishing, warfare, and courtship.

Wampum, strung or woven into headbands, belts, and clothing was exchanged during important occasions. It was presented as gifts to a prospective bride's family, offered to a murder victim's family as restitution, used as a stake in gambling, buried with the dead and presented to the grieving family, and worn as a prestigious ornament. From time to time, it was used to conclude a peace treaty, to celebrate a friendship, or to welcome strangers as was the case when Verrazano and Hudson arrived.

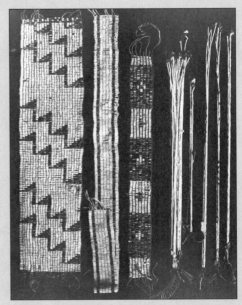

The local Indians used intricately beaded wampum as money.

one shore to the other to come and see us.[1]

Verrazano returned to France, and although he reported his findings he failed to stir further interest in the new bay or the island he had stumbled upon.

Interest in this remote region may have been delayed, but it was not lost. It revived in 1609 when the Englishman Henry Hudson, while sailing his Dutch ship *Halve Maen* (*Half Moon* in English), made the same discovery as Verrazano while seeking a watery passage across North America to China. Unlike his predecessor, however, Hudson remained several weeks exploring the area and, more importantly, drawing accurate maps. What he called the Noort or North River on his map, he later changed to the Hudson River in honor of himself. Before he departed, he claimed the land in the name of the Dutch East India Company, the company that financed his voyage. Although Hudson had failed to find a river passage to China, the furs he brought back showed that there was another reason to return.

New Netherland

Hudson returned to Amsterdam with stories that many thought were wild exaggerations. Dutch entrepreneurs heard about forests that could be harvested for lumber, rivers teeming with fish and beaver, and seemingly limitless stocks of Atlantic fish and shellfish. In 1624

Henry Hudson's Half Moon *sails up the Hudson River past Manhattan.*

thirty Dutch families moved here and immediately established a series of small trading posts and simple towns up and down the Hudson River and named the entire area New Netherland.

The Dutch quickly recognized that the lower tip of Manhattan Island would be the most advantageous location for a city. Docked at this narrow point, ships would be protected from the ravages of Atlantic storms yet close to its waters, they would have easy access to the Hudson River, and the docks could be easily defended from attack. Pleased with the location and the potential for growth and profitable trade, the Dutch named the small emerging city New Amsterdam.

By 1626 Peter Minuit, director general of New Netherland, recognized the importance of the small town of New Amsterdam and made a successful offer to purchase from the Indians the entire ninety-eight-hundred-acre island the Dutch called Manhattes. Though no deed of sale survives, the sale was mentioned in a letter written by a Dutch merchant reporting what he had heard from ship passengers departing from New Netherland. According to the merchant, the West India Company had "Purchased the Island Manhattes from the Indians for the value of 60 guilders [Dutch currency]."[2]

Following the purchase, friction with Indian tribes erupted from time to time north of New Amsterdam. Fortunately for both parties, clever diplomacy gen-

Hudson's Risks and Hardships

When Henry Hudson sailed into New York Harbor in 1609, his third major voyage of discovery, he took many risks and accepted many hardships as the price to be paid for success. Today, all New Yorkers are able to gaze at this great harbor and city and enjoy the city thanks to the difficulties endured by Henry Hudson.

After three days anchored in New York Harbor, Hudson sent his son to measure the depth of the waters about twelve miles up the Hudson River. During the exploration, twenty-six Indians in two canoes attacked the group. His son was killed when an arrow shot into his throat. Hudson buried his son at sea.

One month later, while still scouting the region, the *Half Moon* stopped to trade with some natives. One native came over the rail of the ship and stole clothes, and another attempting to climb aboard was killed by the ship's cook. The *Half Moon* weighed anchor and fled fearing retaliation from the Indians. Two days later the ship was ambushed by Indians, costing lives on both sides. Discouraged and disheartened by the dissension, deaths, and hardships, Hudson eventually returned to England convinced that his sacrifices had yielded nothing more than a failed expedition.

Henry Hudson suffered many hardships while exploring the New York region.

erally resolved the disputes and for the next forty years or so the Dutch settlers thrived and prospered.

Enter the English

The English proved a greater threat to the Dutch than the Indians. English colonies were prospering both north and south of New Amsterdam. Aware of the threat, around the mid-1650s the Dutch fortified their little settlement that occupied the tip of Manhattes. They erected a wooden wall that stretched across the tip

Seal of New Netherland

from one bank to the other, establishing a fortified northern boundary for the city. This wall followed the same line as today's Wall Street.

By 1664 both the Dutch and English were preparing for war. King Charles of England granted his brother, James, the duke of York, vast American territories that included all of New Netherland. James raised a small fleet and sent it to capture New Amsterdam. Dutch director general Peter Stuyvesant, without a fleet or any organized army to defend the colony, was forced to surrender without a struggle. In September of that year, after a mere forty years or so, New Amsterdam was renamed New York in honor of the duke of York.

Today, more than one hundred years later, some evidence of the Dutch remains. The main Dutch influences that visitors see are a few examples of Dutch architecture, a smattering of Dutch street names that the English failed to change, and an occasional splash of Dutch folk culture still found in the art

15

Manhattan's Bill of Sale

No legal document recording the sale of Manhattan by the Lenape to the Dutch exists. The only document of any kind that describes the land sale was a letter written in Amsterdam, Holland, on November 5, 1626, by Pieter Jansen Schagen. He was a deputy to the states general in the Netherlands and his letter remains the only record of the original Dutch purchase. A facsimile of his letter can be found in the article, "The Dutch West Indies Company":

High Mighty Sirs:

Here arrived yesterday the ship *The Arms of Amsterdam* which sailed from New Netherland out of the Mauritius [Hudson] River on September 23; they reported that our people there are of good courage, and live peaceably. Their women, also, have borne children there, they have bought the island Manhattes from the wild men for the value of sixty guilders, is 11,000 morgens [a Dutch measure of land] in extent. They sowed all their grain in the middle of May, and harvested it in the middle of August. Thereof being samples of summer grain, such as wheat, rye, barley, oats, buckwheat, canary seed, small beans, and flax. The cargo of the aforesaid ship is: 7246 beaver skins, 178.5 otter [half] skins, 675 [full] otter skins, 48 mink skins, 36 wild-cat skins, 33 mink, 34 rat skins. Many logs of oak and nut-wood.

Herewith be ye High Mighty Sirs, commended to the Almighty's grace, In Amsterdam, November 5, Anno 1626.

Your High Might's Obedient,

P. Schagen

Peter Minuit purchases Manhattan from the Lenape with furs and wampum.

The first English municipal governor is inaugurated on the steps of New Amsterdam's old state house in 1664. In the same year, the city was renamed New York.

and music of a small number of local taverns, ale houses, and coffee manors.

By the 1680s the influx of English merchants and traders quickened the pace of New York. Ten to fifteen ocean-going freighters crossed the Atlantic each year carrying all manner of household goods to the colonists in exchange for wheat, beaver furs, lumber, corn, and salted fish. It came as no surprise to anyone that merchants involved with trade

became the wealthiest class in the city. Although the English Crown controlled New York, many Dutch remained in the city and their resentment of English rule and the preferential treatment accorded English merchants festered as a growing divisive issue in the still young city.

Repressive British Rule

Friction between the Dutch and English officials of New York increased by

the turn of the century. Only Englishmen were allowed to purchase large tracts of land in the areas surrounding New York and allowed to control local elections even though many Dutch continued to live in the city. Gangs of disaffected citizens took to the streets in protest of what they perceived to be laws strangling non-English townspeople. In 1691 minor acts of civil disobedience prompted the Crown to send troops to the city to quell the "rabble."

Fortunately for the English, flourishing trade offset the civil discord. By the 1720s trade increased in volume and variety. In addition to fish, lumber, wheat, corn, and furs as major commodities shipped to Europe, New York merchants added tons of sugar, molasses, and rum, all refined from sugar cane imported from the Caribbean. By 1750 New York was a thriving port whose shipping had in-

creased tenfold since 1680, and by 1760 it quadrupled again to nearly six hundred ships annually.

New York was acquiring the look and refinement of a miniature London. Merchant ships returning from Europe were loaded to the gunwales with luxury items to decorate the homes of the well-to-do merchant class: elegantly painted porcelain, beautifully crafted and lacquered mahogany furniture, colorful silks, aromatic spices, and fine English tea to serve at the traditional high tea ceremony.

The mercantile success and affluence in New York did not escape the gaze of King George III. He was in constant search of new sources of revenue to finance his costly lifestyle and incessant wars against the French and Spanish. New taxes soon took a bite out of all New Yorkers' pocketbooks, including the

This illustration of the early New Amsterdam skyline reveals its Dutch architectural influence. Since the British assumed control of the city, it has grown dramatically.

pocketbooks of English colonists. One tax led to another until most New Yorkers, along with Bostonians and Philadelphians, were being bled by taxes on a never ending assortment of critical imports, including sugar and tea, which were the most heavily taxed commodities. Additional taxes were levied in the form of stamps, which were actually permits to own businesses, to marry, to publish newspapers, to purchase land, and for dozens of other activities.

In 1765, from the lower tip of Manhattan to expanding areas north of Wall Street and all along the docks, both Dutch and English demonstrators angered by the heavy-handed taxes took to the streets to vent their anger. They ransacked the home of the English mayor who had foolishly sworn in public to "Cram the Stamps down their Throats with the end of my Sword."[3] Acts of defiance spread throughout the city while rebellious New Yorkers formed the Sons of Liberty, a secret patriotic group aimed at overthrowing English tyranny.

War and Victory

At the end of 1765 the Sons of Liberty temporarily shut down the port of New York. Other acts of rebellion followed that included pelting English magistrates with eggs and unsold smelly fish, refusing to purchase English goods, and occasional brawling between seamen swinging cutlasses and clubs against bayonet-wielding English soldiers. One English official reported mobs running through the streets, "Throwing Squibbs [verbal insults], Crackers [contemptuous name calling], firing muskets and pistols, breaking some windows and forcing Knockers off the Doors."[4]

Relations between the Crown and colonists teetered on the edge of war. In March 1770 New York's Sons of Liberty learned of the Boston Massacre where English troops killed five and wounded eight Boston patriots; and again in 1773 they learned that the Boston Sons of Liberty, led by John Adams, boarded and dumped hundreds of chests of English tea into Boston Harbor. In 1774, in sympathy with their fellow patriots, New Yorkers sent delegates to the First Continental Congress, secretly meeting in Philadelphia, at which the right of the colonies to break from the king and assert their independence was affirmed.

By 1775 the inevitable war was on. King George III dispatched an additional ten thousand troops to New York to crush the rebellion. What happened after the English took control of New York is common knowledge to all New Yorkers. Over the course of eight years, several battles were fought in the surrounding townships but none of any consequence in New York City; English troops heavily occupied the city, forcing residents to flee.

Eventually, after a series of seesaw battles, General Washington moved his troops to Yorktown in 1781 and soundly defeated General Cornwallis. On October 19, a substantial English army surrendered to Washington, breaking the English will to continue the war. On September 3, 1783, the peace treaty was signed.

New Yorkers were among the most vocal protesters of unfair colonial taxes in the years before the Revolutionary War.

General Cornwallis surrenders to General Washington. New York was heavily damaged during the war, but the city is now almost fully rebuilt.

America's Finest City Rebuilds

On September 4, 1783, New Yorkers got down to the business of rebuilding America's Finest City. Eight years of enemy occupation, bombardments from their cannons, and terrible fires reduced New York to rubble. New York writer William Dewar, who experienced the war years, recalled that the skeletal walls of gutted buildings, "Cast their grim shadows upon the pavement, imparting an unearthly aspect to the streets."[5] James Duane returned the day the English evacuated the city and found two of his houses looking, "as if they had been inhabited by savages or wild beasts."[6] Many streets stripped bare of their trees were obstructed by trenches and other fortifications built by the English. Garbage and refuse lay everywhere. Wharves and warehouses had crumbled from years of neglect and fires. The merchant fleet that had not been burned at the wharves had vanished.

Today, just ten years later, New York City has thirty-six thousand residents, the largest population of any American city. As historian James Hardy recalled recently, "The British had scarcely left our city, when order seemed to arise out of confusion."[7]

Chapter 2

Arriving, Location, and Weather

New York is the most energetic city in America. Day and night, the deafening sounds of wagon wheels and horse hooves clatter across the city's slippery cobblestone boulevards. Much of the street traffic consists of wagons carrying goods to awaiting ships. Some well-to-do city dwellers travel the streets in fashionable four-wheel chaises but many more residents ride horses. Yet most New Yorkers walk in the city which is compact, each neighborhood having a variety of marketplaces and artisan shops.

The fastest, safest, and least expensive way for American vacationers to travel to New York is by overland roads. Boat travel up and down the eastern seaboard is available but not recommended because of violent weather, ruthless pirates, and poorly constructed boats. Instead, travelers visiting New York from the other twelve states should reserve seats on one of several stage lines that link all major cities with New York.

Arriving in New York by Land

For fellow Americans interested in joining New Yorkers for either the Fourth of July or Evacuation Day festivities, a network of roads suitable for horses and wagons leads to the city. Travelers from the larger cities to the south will find reasonably well-maintained roads, especially those connecting to Philadelphia, Williamsburg, and Charleston. The best road to New York, however, is the Boston Post Road, which connects with Boston to the north and dozens of smaller towns and cities in between.

As the name suggests, this road was initially designed for post riders who carry the mail. In 1772 the road was enlarged and improved to accommodate wagon and commercial stagecoach service. Today's travelers can choose to pass through the towns and cities that lie along one of three different routes between Boston and New York. From New

Although you may choose to travel the streets of New York in an elegant horse-drawn carriage, the city is also easily navigated on foot.

York to Boston by commercial coach in good weather is a seven-day adventure.

The advantages to choosing the Post Road over other smaller roads are many. Most evident is the width and smoothness of this road that is sufficient to accommodate carriage and wagon traffic with considerable comfort compared to older and less well-maintained roads. A second reason is safety; the Post Road has a constant flow of travelers to deter highwaymen from robbing travelers. The third good reason is the engineering of the road that accommodates wet winter travel by the placement of flat wood beams laid side by side along the length of the trail and embedded into the road surface. Coaches traveling these roads are less apt to become mired in mud.

Arriving in New York by Boat

Visitors from Europe have no option but to travel to New York by boat. Arriving in New York by boat is a tricky proposition; the city is not visible from the Atlantic, making it difficult to locate. Tucked in and away from the high seas by a narrow six-mile-long inlet called the Narrows, many ships' captains experience great difficulty locating this narrow channel. Ships' captains sailing here, particularly when it is their first voyage, can easily miss it, especially at night and in the fog. When this occurs, and it frequently does, captains find themselves lost and wandering farther north or south of the city.

This protected safe haven is one of the city's many unique geographic assets. Safely huddled away within a sheltered bay, the deep swells and battering waves of the Atlantic are calmed to little more than benign choppy whitecaps by the time they reach the tip of Manhattan. Protected by Long Island along the north coast and Staten Island along the south coast, travelers arriving by boat marvel that Verrazano was able to find New York nearly three centuries ago.

As your sailing vessel approaches the inlet, you will hear the captain order a member of his crew to start "sounding for the bottom." If you have not seen this procedure, it is interesting to watch. A deck-hand appears with a length of rope that has a heavy iron weight attached to one end and a knot tied every fathom, which is the nautical equivalent of six feet. He then drops the weighted end over the side of the ship to test the depth of the water by locating the bottom. Watch the rope play out and you will see it quickly disappear into the dark water until the weight hits bottom. At that moment, the rope is no longer being pulled and it suddenly becomes slack. The deckhand then pulls up the rope counting the number of knots and shouts the depth to the captain.

When the ship's sounding is eight fathoms, the captain knows he should be sighting land soon and slows the ship's speed to search for landmarks that will guide him toward the Narrows into New York. As yet, no lighthouses have been built along the outer coast of New York's harbor although one was approved just this year for construction at the far end of Long Island.

Once the inlet is located, seasoned captains know the bottom sounding is six to seven fathoms, and they must proceed slowly because most large ships draw five fathoms. Unwilling to risk the loss of his ship, your captain may choose the cautious procedure of dropping anchor and sending a small boat ashore to find a local navigator called a pilot. These local mariners know the currents and locations

Frightened Passengers

The passage from Europe to America can be treacherous by any standard. Many of the immigrants now arriving are too poor to pay for the journey and therefore indenture themselves to wealthier New Yorkers by selling their services for a period of years in return for the price of the passage. Crammed into a small wooden ship, rolling and rocking at the mercy of the winds and sea, the voyagers—men, women, and children—endure many hardships and sometimes die at sea. John T. Humphrey, in his article "Traveling to America," provides the following harrowing diary account describing a moment on a 1746 crossing to America:

Black clouds rested heavily on the southern horizon and foretold of an unusually severe storm . . . all port-holes and hatches were closed and fastened, the upper yards were lowered and the sails furled. . . . Soon after 8 o'clock a hurricane broke loose, far more terrible than we dreamed an ocean could be . . . winds howled, roaring waves ran mountains high. . . . All passengers were gathered in the cabins and a solemn stillness reigned . . . about 10 o'clock there was a terrible shock . . . the side of the ship against which my wife was leaning was now the bottom and the bottom had become one of the sides of the cabin and we realized the ship had capsized . . . a cry was raised for axes to cut away the masts . . . the Captain bravely climbed the main mast, and under his blows it parted and went over. Instantly, the ship righted itself and floated on even keel!

Such dramatic accounts were commonplace. Many other diaries describe crossings that included burials at sea and landing at the first sighting of land to bury infant children born but unable to survive the relentless high seas. One group of English that went ashore to bury a dead child encountered a resident who commented on how fit they appeared after such a long voyage. He noted that passengers on most ships usually got a fever and many often perished. He went on to say, according to John T. Humphrey, that "They [the dead] were placed by the scores [twenty at a time] in large ditches near the shore and covered with sand." Statements similar to this one suggest that the remains of many immigrants were perhaps similarly buried on the beaches of New England from Maine to Virginia.

European travelers should prepare for harsh storms during the passage across the Atlantic.

of hidden sandbars. Once found and brought on board, the pilot safely steers your ship up the narrow channel as it slowly makes a right turn toward the first sight of the city's skyline.

First Sighting of the City

The New York skyline comes into view as your ship negotiates several small islands sprinkled about the Upper New York Bay. The largest and the first that comes into view dead ahead is Governors Island followed slightly off to the left by the smaller Bedloe's and Gibbet Islands. As your pilot glides the ship past these islands, it will immediately become evident to everyone that New York City occupies the lower tip of Manhattan Island. The closest major buildings that define the skyline along the shore occupy the area called the Battery. This name derives from a time when the Dutch first arrived and established rows or batteries of cannon here to defend the city. As the ship approaches, Fort George will come into view as the dom-

inant structure that still bristles with cannons.

Just north of the Battery, the rest of New York's skyline snaps into focus. It is characterized by four-story buildings punctuated by occasional church spires. The eight most prominent steeples can be identified behind Fort George. From left to right are: Trinity Church, the Lutheran Church, the New Dutch Church, Saint Paul's Church, Federal Hall, the Old Dutch Church, the Secretary's office in the Battery fort, and the Church in the Fort.

Off to the left and right shores, as Manhattan widens to the north, is the Port of New York. Your ship will make a slight right turn at this point and sail along the east side of the port until it comes to one of the larger docks, probably Albany Pier or Murray's Wharf, or sails slightly farther up the island to the shipyards near Peck's Market. From this vantage point, minutes away from docking, newly arrived guests will begin to get a better feel for Manhattan Island.

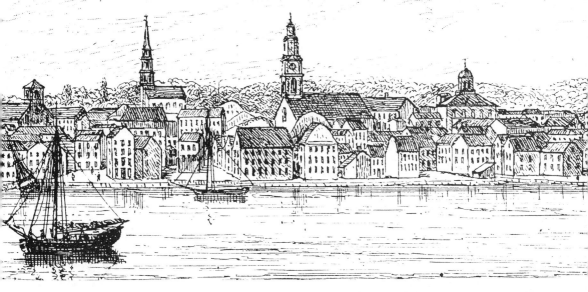

Sailing into New York harbor affords travelers breathtaking views of the city's skyline.

Manhattan Island

As any New Yorker will tell you, Manhattan Island is also New York Island. Although the city itself occupies only the lower tip of Manhattan, as the city grows, it will continue to spread north because it has no where else to expand. Although it is highly unlikely that it will ever spread all the way to Harlem on the northern end, New Yorkers are optimistic that more growth is still to come.

Manhattan Island is unlike any other. It is long and narrow, roughly thirteen miles along its north-south axis and two miles wide. That is not so unusual but the way it is surrounded by water certainly is. Down the west side of Manhattan flows the Hudson River on its journey to the sea. The Hudson is still called the North River by many old-time Dutch sailors who sit on barrels along the Battery smoking their long white clay pipes. Along the north and northeast sides of the island flows the Harlem River that connects with a small channel of the Hudson to flow eastward into the Atlantic Ocean.

The last segment of water surrounding the island flows along most of the east side of Manhattan in a very narrow spit of saltwater that sweeps in from the Atlantic amid a scatter of small islands. This channel is so narrow that it has the appearance of being a river and for that reason most New Yorkers refer to it as the "East River" even though it is a narrow saltwater strait. Looking at the East River, one can see water flowing both north and south at the same time because of the unusual currents from the ocean flowing amidst the many islands. Along the southern tip where New York sits, the water is a brackish mix of saltwater from the Atlantic and freshwater from the Hudson River.

Although thirty-six thousand residents occupy only the lower end of the island—no more than 5 percent of the

27

island—the remainder of the land is used as the city's breadbasket and summer vacation retreat. Available to country dwellers are small rustic plots used for farms, orchards, pastureland, sources of fresh pond and well water, and light timber harvesting. As the city grows in the future, it will undoubtedly encompass more of the northern rural farms in the area presently called the "out country."

Wall Street

Wall Street is a short yet historically significant street. The street takes its unusual yet descriptive name from either 1652 or 1653 when fear of a possible Indian or English attack prompted the Dutch to build a wall from water's edge to water's edge.

When the wall was completed, it stood twelve feet high and eighteen inches thick. Interspaced along the length of the wall were five stone bastions used as lookout towers and as battlements for Dutch defenders. The wall was never tested in battle and in 1699 the English dismantled it yet named the street running parallel to the wall, Wall Street.

Today the street is beginning to develop a new reputation. Anchored close to the docks on the East River, Wall Street is the home of several business ventures catering to shippers, buyers and sellers of cargo, marine insurance companies, the slave market, and financial speculators willing to lend money to developing businesses in need of money. Of potentially greater interest, stocks in a small number of companies began trading five or six years ago near the large buttonwood tree where Queen and Wall Streets intersect.

New York Weather

The weather in New York, along with the city's commerce, is affected by its proximity to the ocean. The Atlantic Ocean provides a temperate climate that is generally warm in the summer, usually in the middle to high seventies, but not insufferably hot. In winter, the temperature drops on average to the mid-thirties.

The winds also play a role in determining the weather. New York occasionally receives sharp winter blasts that seem to come down the Hudson River. During the spring and summer, warm gentle winds seem to arrive from Virginia and the Carolinas. These warmer winds, which visit New York in the late summer months, can carry moisture that makes the air feel sticky. Occasionally, however, when these warm humid winds mix with the cooler breezes coming off the Atlantic, the warm yet crisp feel of the air creates a festive atmosphere drawing all New Yorkers out onto the streets to enjoy the refreshing weather.

Without a doubt, the best time to visit America's Finest City is during the annual Independence Day celebration on the fourth of July. This festive occasion occurs right in the middle of the best season to visit New York—May through October, with late spring and early autumn being the most pleasant.

A Safe City

New York is both a large and safe city for vacationers. For example, a severe fire has never ravaged the city. There are

New York City and its harbor are visible from upper Manhattan Island. Visitors should make time to tour this charming, rustic countryside.

several reasons for this excellent safety record. High on the list, and the oldest reason, is because of the "rattle watch." A group of men patrol the city night and day on the lookout for fires. When one is spotted, they sound the alarm with large wood and metal rattles that emit a distinctively loud warning.

A second reason is the professional fire department. Established in 1778 as the Fire Department of New York, the department presently numbers 367 men, all of whom are required by law to be "Strong, able, discreet, honest, and sober men."[8] These firefighters are charged with the deployment of twelve horse-drawn pumpers,

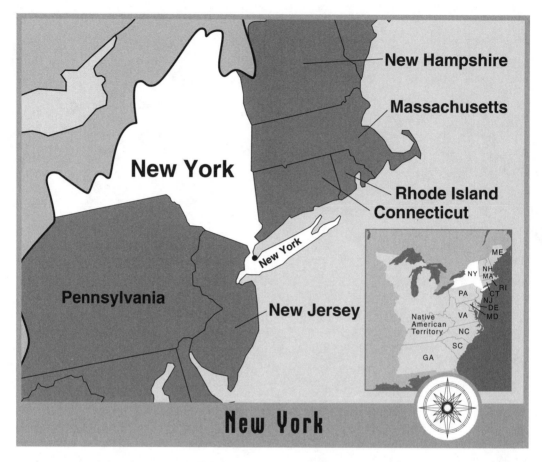

New Hampshire

Massachusetts

New York

Rhode Island
Connecticut

New York

Pennsylvania

New Jersey

ME
NY NH
MA
PA RI
CT
NJ
DE
Native VA MD
American
Territory NC
SC
GA

New York

each operated by four men. When the pumpers come upon a fire, the firemen drop leather hoses into wells, ponds, or the wharf, and by furiously pumping wooden handles they are capable of forcing water though the leather hoses high enough to reach a three-story building. The leather hoses initially leak a great deal because of the stitching that binds long sections together, but once the leather swells from the moisture, the leaks decrease. In addition to the professional firemen, every citizen is required by law to respond to fires with buckets in hand.

Other reasons that so few fires plague New York include the city's fireboat and several forty-foot-tall circular fire towers strategically scattered about the city. Because wharf fires are capable of destroying boats as well as structures, New York is the only city in America with a fireboat fitted with pumps capable of fighting fires from the water.

The office of the fire warden established in 1791 to inspect structures has also reduced fires. The city authorized each of the seven districts, called wards, to appoint a fire warden authorized to enter all houses and businesses to check fireplaces and stoves and to make certain that each had its required number of leather fire buckets. Just this year, in order to assist fire crews and citizens to locate fires and other emergencies more quickly, the city passed a law requiring systematic house numbering as well as direction boards posting the name of streets on wood signs bolted to buildings.

In addition to a fire-safe city, locals also like to boast about the safety of their streets. New York, like London, has two sets of law enforcement officers

New York City's professional fire department is prepared to extinguish any blaze, making the city one of the safest in America.

that patrol the city's streets. The constables patrol the streets during the day to keep order, and they are identifiable by their badges, hats, and the five-foot-long wood staffs they carry for defense. On one end of the staff is a round solid brass knob used for cracking heads when necessary. During the night, the constables are replaced by the night watch that serves the same function.

In addition to the armed patrols, ever since the war all of the major streets have become safer at night because of the addition of lamps set on eight-foot-

Profiting from the Cold

Cold winters have created opportunities for many New York entrepreneurs. The ponds that can be found north of the city at the upper end of Manhattan freeze during the winter months. Just before the thaw begins in early spring, ice harvesters cut blocks of ice and store them in icehouses where the blocks are packed in layers of sawdust and straw for later summer sale to New York residents and businesses to keep foods and drinks cool and fresh.

The ice-harvesting process first requires men to scrape the snow away from the pond surface. The next step is to cut deep grooves through the ice behind horses pulling a large iron knife until the blocks break off. Then, using bars and one-handed crosscut ice saws, workmen finish cutting the blocks of ice and float them to a chute where they are hauled inside for storage. Once the blocks are stored inside, the icehouse is heavily layered and surrounded by sawdust and straw supplied as insulation.

It is widely known that George Washington has his own private icehouse and that Thomas Jefferson has one at Monticello that is sixteen feet deep, capable of holding sixty-two wagon loads of block ice.

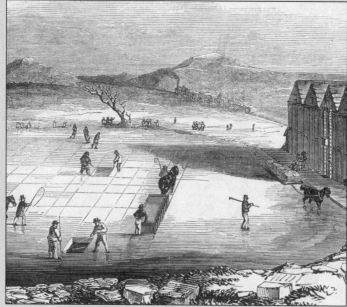

Horse-drawn blades cut ice from frozen ponds in upper Manhattan.

With modern streetlamps and constables on patrol, visitors can stroll safely and comfortably along most New York streets.

tall posts. Each evening as the night watch begins its patrol, each member ignites the whale-oil lamps in his ward and extinguishes them in the morning when he is relieved by a constable.

All things considered, New York is a safe place for a vacation. Once you arrive and find a good inn, a bite to eat, and become acquainted with the city's layout, you will begin to feel right at home.

Chapter 3

First Day: Getting Around and Where to Eat

A s soon as vacationers arrive, they recognize that the lifeblood of the city is its docks. Surrounded by water on three sides, the smell of salt air is as constant and pervasive as the energy of the city that never seems to sleep. Bristling like spines on a sea urchin, docks prick the water's edge from the upper East River shipyards, down and around the Battery, and back up again along the Hudson River to King's Wharf.

One of the simple joys of the docks is their unmistakable and pleasurable smells. At any time on any day New Yorkers and visitors stroll the docks and look with astonishment at more than a hundred seagoing billowed freighters. Take in the exotic aromas of coffee beans from the West Indies, chests of teas originating in India and Cathay, and sacks of aromatic spices that began their journey on the backs of camels across the Arabian desert.

The continuous stream of freighters putting into port keeps the wharves alive twenty-four hours a day. Dozens of different types of craftsmen such as carpenters, joiners, caulkers, riggers, blacksmiths, anchor makers, and sail and rope makers are hard at work. Joining the craftsmen are gangs of common laborers called stevedores who load and unload cargo from around the world. According to the English traveler William Strickland, just last year

more [ships] than I ever saw, except on the Thames below London Bridge. Bales of cotton, wool, and merchandise;

At New York's docks, visitors experience a variety of exotic sights, sounds, and smells. Here, new arrivals may also hire a cart for transport to a local inn.

barrels of potash, rice, flour, and salt provisions; hogsheads of sugar, chests of tea, puncheons of rum, and pipes of wine; boxes, cases, packs, and packages of all sizes and denominations, were strewn upon the wharfs and landing places, or upon the decks of the shipping."[9]

Wandering along some of the smaller docks it becomes evident that the abundance of the sea also plays a major role in the life of the city. Being tossed from small fishing boats to the docks amidst the hollering of the fishermen are baskets filled with a variety of squirming sea life. Varieties include oysters, crabs, clams, scallops, mussels, and lobsters. All of this bounty is sorted, weighed, and tossed into baskets that will shortly be picked up by carters and hauled off to taverns and marketplaces throughout the city.

For those of you arriving with large sea chests, suitcases, and leather boxes, these same carters can help you. Keep an eye peeled for one of them. For a small price a carter will put your goods into his cart and transport them to your inn. Carters are easily recognized by their white frock coat, a tattered farmer's hat, and long clay pipe. These men are licensed to carry goods throughout the city, but be sure to negotiate the cost before engaging their services. While they carry your goods, use the opportunity to

Baskets of fresh fish and other seafood are unloaded every morning at the city's waterfront landings.

question them about the city. No one knows New York's interesting spots and secret back streets better than these hardworking men.

Getting Around the City

The streets of New York resemble those of medieval Amsterdam. This is not surprising, since the Dutch influence dates back more than 150 years. Local historians agree that most of New York's streets and roads are nearly identical to those in Amsterdam; crooked, narrow, made of rough cobblestone, and adjacent to water. Besides the Dutch influence, local old-timers say that whenever possible, today's major roads were intentionally constructed to follow Indian trails. These old trails, established hundreds of years ago, were the easiest routes over the uneven terrain, across Manhattan's many small streams, and around several ponds.

The only roads that appear to be planned in any way are the major thoroughfares in and out of the city that run north-south. These boulevards include Broadway, Broad Street, Queen Street, and Nassau Street.

Of some assistance to first-time visitors is the geographic division of the city into wards. Presently New York has seven wards with names and numbers but the names are never used. Fortunately, their numerical ordering ascends from south to north. If, for example, someone gives you directions to find a street or venue of interest in ward number one, you will know to head all the way to the lower end of the city somewhere between Wall Street and the Battery. As an additional bit of advice, purchase a modern map of the city at any of the city's many bookstores. Recommended is either the one drawn by

Wall Street is one of the more pleasant thoroughfares in New York. Many of the city's other streets are crooked and narrow.

Shoppers make their way through the crowd at Liberty and William Streets. Getting around the cobbled streets of New York can be difficult without a good map.

Taylor and Roberts or the one by Ratzer called the "Plan of New York." Of the two, the Ratzer map is the more comprehensive.

Although most any place in New York is within walking distance of any other part of the city, those pressed for time or simply wishing to remain dry during wet weather can hire a private carriage for service along all major roads. At the ma-

jor intersections you will see black carriages with yellow lettering down the side identifying them as Asa Hall's Stage Line. For twenty-five cents, these convenient horse-drawn covered carriages will take you anywhere in the city.

New York Ferries

Bounded by water, every New Yorker depends on ferries to get around the city and to the many small islands just off the southern point of Manhattan. Today's ferries are propelled either by oar or sail, and occasionally by a combination of the two. The most distinctive vessel you will see is a small sailing sloop called a "periauger," meaning a boat that goes around islands. The majority of ferryboat docks are located along the East River. All of these take you south down to the Battery and even around the southern point of Manhattan and north up the east side along the Hudson River. The farthest north any ferries venture is to the Paulus Hook ferry landing at the foot of Cortlandt Street, just a three-or four-block walk from Broadway. Although the ride is an exciting way to take in the view of New York's colorful wharves, it is sometimes faster and cheaper to simply walk across the city.

These same wharves also handle ferryboats to most islands. The ferry to Long Island, for example, departs hourly from the dock at the foot of Crown Street where it meets Burnets Key at the water's edge. If, on the other hand, you wish to explore Staten or Governors Island, go down to the Battery to the most southern point where the Whitehall Slip is located. Once there, just ask the ticket seller which ferry is going to which island. A round-trip ticket to Staten Island is five cents and

tickets for Governors Island are three cents each.

So much walking and exploring can make any tourist hungry. For those who are new to the city, taverns are the most congenial places to eat, make new friends, and to learn from locals what New York has to offer.

Taverns

Taverns, commonly called "grog shops" by sailors and "tippling houses" by prominent New Yorkers, abound throughout the city. Tired, thirsty, and hungry sightseers have more taverns to choose from than in any other city in America; 468 to be exact, at least that is the current number of tavern licenses issued by the city manager. The number is high in part because of the city's twenty rum distilleries, in part because taverns function as the center of social life for most New Yorkers, and in part because of an unusually high number of young single men who work the wharves.

More than half of the city's taverns are scattered about the lower part of Manhattan, and depending upon your travel budget, you will be able to find places offering suitable fare from a simple bite to eat accompanied by a tankard of ale, to a gourmet meal washed down with fine French wine. For those without

The Streets and Buildings of New York

The streets of lower Manhattan and the buildings on them make little sense to first-time travelers to New York. Although most streets are straight, many careen off at odd angles rather than intersecting at right angles. Many European visitors have been critical of the layout of the city and its architecture.

According to historians Anne-Marie Cantwell and Dianna di Zerega Wall in their book *Unearthing Gotham: The Archaeology of New York City,* the English traveler James Birket commented in 1750,

Neither their streets nor houses are at all Regular. Some being 4 or 5 stories & Others not above two, Not any of the Modern houses are built with the Gable End to the Street as was formerly the fashion amongst all the old Dutch Settlers, but are many of 'em Spacious Genteel Houses. Some are built of hewn stone Others of English & also of the Small white Hollands Brick, which looks neat but not grand, their houses are Generally neat within and well Furnished. The Streets are very Irregular & Crooked & many of 'em much too Narrow they are Generally pretty well paved which adds much to the decency & Cleanness of the place & the Advantages of Carriage.

Also, according to Cantwell and Wall, James Boardman, a visitor from Liverpool, England, remarked,

The main street called Broadway, is two miles and a half long, in a straight line, and proportionally wide, with broad flagging trottoirs, or side-walks some parts of which are shaded by poplars and other lofty trees; but in the quarter devoted to business, canvas blinds are stretched from the shops to permanent wooden rails of a convenient height and neatly finished. The architecture of the buildings, however, does not at all correspond with the magnificent scale of the street, the greatest irregularity prevailing; handsome edifices of brick, and even marble, of four and five stories, being side by side with those of two and three, and in some parts actually intermixed with miserable wooden cottages.

much of an appetite, taverns can still be spirited and colorful places to have a drink, with or without alcohol, meet friends, trade gossip, argue politics, or find a job.

Elaborately carved and vividly painted signs mounted in front of each tavern direct you to the front door. The most notable taverns, because of their artistically designed signs that graphically and colorfully depict their names, are the Black Horse, White Lion, Blue Bell, and St. George and the Dragon. There is more to the signs than meets the eye. Since most citizens are illiterate, the colors and designs of these vivid picture signs assist everyone in locating their favorite tavern.

At the center of activity in most taverns stands the large welcoming fireplace that heats the establishment through the winter. The fireplace in finer taverns also serves as the roasting spit for beef, venison, ham, wild boar, large fowl, and Atlantic cod. Moving farther into the heart of the tavern, vacationers always marvel at some of the finer bars crafted from beautiful long planks of ebony, mahogany, and oak. Behind the bar, locked in cabinets, patrons will find the finer spirits. Common drinks such as ales, rum, chocolate, and apple cider are drawn by hand pumps directly from barrels under the bar. Because of these levers that are pulled down to draw the drink, locals simply call for a "pull of ale" or a "pull of cider."

The finest taverns, such as the luxurious Fraunces Tavern on Pearl Street, also provide side rooms exclusively for the use of gentlemen. These rooms offer additional social activities such as billiards, cigar smoking, dart games, and poker.

Working-class taverns frequented by sailors and dockworkers are far more basic. At the corner of Water and Ferry Streets you cannot miss a tavern sign with a carving of a large yellow and green pineapple. Welcome to the Pine

Ferryboats are available at Whitehall Slip to take adventurous travelers to the islands surrounding Manhattan. Ferries to other destinations are available along the East River.

& Apple. Platters of corned beef, sharp cheddar cheese, sliced Bermuda onions, and stacks of salty crackers satisfy every appetite. Lacking chairs, eating and drinking are done standing up. This is also a good place to find work on the docks and wager on cockfighting on Sunday afternoons. In addition, a bed by the stove can be had for a nickel.

Coffeehouses

Sightseers looking for a quieter place where they can sit and talk about the day's activities or tomorrow's planned sightseeing might be interested in spending an hour or two at one of the city's coffeehouses. Since the Revolution, young professionals aspiring to be men of letters as well as professional successes

Tavern patrons enjoy drinks and lively conversation before a roaring fire. New York has hundreds of taverns, offering food and accommodation in all price ranges.

The Fraunces Tavern, one of New York's oldest and grandest establishments, is on Pearl Street near the Battery.

have been frequenting the coffeehouses of the city. Coffeehouses also accommodate women clientele.

On Broadway, just one block north of Trinity Church, the King's Arms is New York's most well known coffeehouse. It is known to attract genteel regulars interested in discussing politics, travel to Europe and South America, the latest cultural attractions, and the financial future of New York. Coffeehouses are not common in New York, but among the city's social elite they are favorite places for escaping the city's unrefined rabble, derisively called the "hoi polloi" by polite society.

Before the war the King's Arms provided a secret meeting place for the Sons of Liberty. This is not the only coffeehouse of such historical importance in New York. Another coffeehouse, Burn's Coffee House, was also a meeting place for the Sons of Liberty who posted broadsides around the city in 1775 with the banner headline, LIBERTY, PROPERTY, AND NO STAMPS. Down at the end of Wall Street, a room in the Tontine Coffee

Fraunces Tavern and the War

Fraunces Tavern is the most historically significant tavern in New York. Located on the corner of Queen and Canal Streets, it began serving customers in 1719 as the Sign of Queen Charlotte Tavern, named after the wife of King George III. In 1762 the tavern was purchased by the West Indian innkeeper Samuel Fraunces. Because of its location, it quickly became a social center for leaders of shipping, finance, and politics in New York and served as a fashionable meeting place for colonists before the war.

By the early 1770s the political climate had dramatically changed. As tensions between New Yorkers and the English Crown approached a violent climax, Fraunces decided that it was time to put the tavern up for sale. Although he failed to find a buyer, he did succeed in acquiring the friendship of George Washington who visited the tavern frequently. The tavern soon became known as a meeting place for those who opposed the Crown, and it was here that leaders of the revolution, the Sons of Liberty, held their clandestine meetings to discuss their plans for the future. Fraunces showed his support for the group led by Washington by changing the tavern's English name to simply, "Fraunces Tavern."

When the war ended, Fraunces Tavern hosted Washington and his officers in a victory banquet. On December 4, 1783, General Washington returned to the tavern to recite a very emotional farewell speech to his officers in the Long Room.

After the war, the tavern housed offices of the Continental Congress specified in the Articles of Confederation. With the establishment of the Constitution and the inauguration of Washington as president in 1789, Fraunces Tavern became one of the first buildings to be occupied by offices of the federal government agencies, including the departments of Foreign Affairs, Treasury, and War.

General George Washington says good-bye to his loyal officers at the Fraunces Tavern.

House serves as the office for the nascent New York Stock Exchange.

Eating on the Go

Since coffeehouses do not serve food and taverns do not always offer the right atmosphere for travelers, the better alternative might be a quick snack while exploring the streets of New York. Tourists whose travel style is to be on the move at all times can find tasty fare at one of the city's many outdoor public markets. The best for finding a quick snack, or for shopping for dinner, are Catherine's Market near Catherine Slip, Fly Market at the foot of Maiden Lane where it meets Queen Street, and Peck's Market at Peck's Slip and Water Street.

Each marketplace is actually three small markets: one for meats, one for country-grown produce, and the third for fish. The best market and the one with the most character is Fly Market. Here the foods are set out on tables smack in the middle of the street forcing pedestrians and horse-drawn carriages to go around. On the tables, hungry pedestrians are free to pick whatever looks interesting. Wicker baskets are piled high with a variety of small and large loaves of bread, bushel baskets filled with apples and berries, glass jars with dried spiced strips of meat called "jerky," copper and pewter flagons of beer and New York's finest rum, ceramic bowls filled with quarter-

pound pieces of smoked cod, trays of fresh raw and steamed oysters, and shaded baskets of bite-sized chunks of chocolate from the West Indies selling for a half a cent each.

One interesting vendor here sells a thin flat cake, about the size of a teacup saucer, cooked in a pan over an open fire. The Native Americans taught settlers how to prepare these cakes using batter made from cornmeal, milk, and eggs. To make them tastier, the women cooking them pour a stream of maple syrup over

Fresh oysters are available at most outdoor markets.

Fixed Meals

Ordinaries, which are restaurants similar to taverns, dish up a variety of foods for hundreds of New Yorkers each day. Unlike taverns, however, ordinaries serve a fixed menu for each of the seven days of the week, at a fixed price, and at fixed times. An example of this sort of "fixed dining" is in the article "New York Ordinaries," which provides the following colorful and detailed advertisement for an ordinary owned by New Yorker William Sykes:

William Sykes respectfully acquaints the public, that his new dining-rooms, being now completed, the ORDINARY will commence on Tuesday, the 7th. Dinner on the table at 3 o'clock precisely. Price 50¢, including table liquors, or 12 dinner tickets for five dollars and twenty-five cents. The table will always be covered with an ample variety of the delicacies of the season; and Merchants, Brokers, and others, may rely on the utmost punctuality with respect to time, which can be obtained, will be afforded. The bill of fare may be seen in the bar every day at 12 o'clock. A saddle of venison will be served at the Ordinary every Tuesday and Friday at 3 o'clock, and on Sundays at 2 o'clock. On the alternate days, hashed venison, and other esteemed dishes, will be added to the ordinary provision for the public table.

A second table will be covered at 4 o'clock every day, for the accommodation of those gentlemen whose avocations do not permit them to dine at an earlier hour. The dinner will consist of meats removed from the ordinary, but served up anew, with hot vegetables; Price 25¢, or 12 tickets for 2 dollars and fifty cents.

The Coffee Room, which is commodiously and handsomely fitted up, will be daily furnished with a bill of fare, and gentlemen can dine at any hour, upon very short notice. The Larder will be constantly supplied with every delicacy of the New York, Philadelphia, and other markets.

Private rooms for parties, and Dinners, Suppers etc. furnished in the best style. Wines and Liquors, of superior quality, and genuine as imported. Oyster, Terraplo, Ox Tail, Gravy or Peas Soup, every day at 11 o'clock.

Restaurants known as ordinaries serve fixed-menu dinners twice daily, every day of the week.

Strips of beef jerky dry over a smoky fire. New York markets also sell hot corncakes and fresh fruit for a quick meal on the go.

the top and they are delicious all by themselves. For one cent, they are worth a try. These same women also sell a warm brown bread made from wheat flour, molasses, eggs, and a sprinkle of cinnamon.

There is no need to be concerned about the quality or quantity of the foods you purchase because city regulators patrol the markets daily to ensure honest business practices. The city weighmaster checks each merchant's scale to guarantee that the weight of all purchases is accurate. The gaugemaster inspects measuring sticks and measuring bowls for accuracy, and the health inspector smells and inspects meats and fish for freshness.

With all of this information about how New York operates and how to negotiate the streets, docks, and alleyways, it is time for everyone to plan his or her itinerary. For history buffs and for those who have come here out of patriotic respect for the role New York played in the recent war, spending one day visiting historic landmarks will be a memorable experience.

Chapter 4

Five Historic Landmarks

Much of the history of New York can be experienced by visiting some of the city's historical landmarks. Historians will be especially interested in seeing some of the places that General Washington visited during the war and the places President Washington visited after his inauguration. Five historical stops that are of interest have been geographically organized so walkers can comfortably see them in one day. Begin at the southernmost landmark, Fort George, move north to Trinity Church, then Federal Hall, Saint Paul's Church, and finally Columbia College.

NEW NETHERLAND
From the Map of
A. VANDERDONCK
1656.

Fort George

The defense of New York began with the founding of the city by the Dutch at a time when the city's name was still New Amsterdam. Fittingly, the first fort, built at the lower tip of Manhattan at what is today the Battery, was christened Fort Amsterdam in 1624. Since then, it has been rebuilt, strengthened, and renamed several times until becoming Fort George under English rule. The reason the name remains English is because the fort is scheduled for demolition next year and there is no point in changing it.

Once Manhattan Island was chosen as the center of the New Netherland colony, the choice of location for the fort was obvious. It would be, as Adriaen Van der Donck wrote in 1649, twenty-five years after it had been built, "in the south point of Manhattan Island, at the junction of the East and North rivers."[10]

The purpose for the fort, he went on to explain was, "not only to close and command the said rivers but to possess as well all the lands comprehended between them as round about them."[11]

Visitors to the three-story brick fort enter through a well-protected set of thick oak doors studded with iron bolts to prevent the door from being sawed or chopped down with axes. Inside, the fort consists of a large central courtyard used for drilling and training the six-hundred-man garrison and for stacking cannon-balls and other supplies. Around the perimeter, deep within the thirty-foot-thick brick walls are the soldiers' quarters, mess hall, infirmary, and a variety of store-rooms. On the top two levels, students of history will find the fort's ninety-two cannons, the majority of which are aimed toward the harbor. Each cannon is capable of firing either a thirty-two- or a sixty-four-pound iron ball, depending upon the diameter of its barrel.

On Evacuation Day, November 25, 1783, a detail of patriots went to the

Fort George has been located at the tip of Manhattan since the days of old New Amsterdam. Visitors should tour this historical landmark before it is demolished.

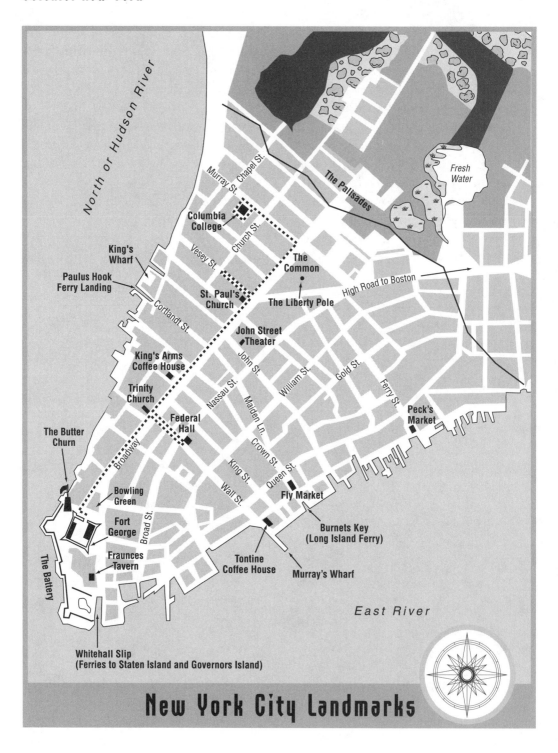

North or Hudson River

The Palisades

Fresh Water

Murray St.

Chapel St.

Columbia College

Church St.

Vesey St.

King's Wharf

The Common

Paulus Hook Ferry Landing

Cortlandt St.

St. Paul's Church

The Liberty Pole

High Road to Boston

John Street Theater

John St.

King's Arms Coffee House

Nassau St.

William St.

Gold St.

Ferry St.

Trinity Church

Maiden Ln.

Peck's Market

Federal Hall

The Butter Churn

Broadway

Crown St.

Queen St.

Bowling Green

King St.

Fly Market

Fort George

Wall St.

Broad St.

Burnets Key (Long Island Ferry)

The Battery

Fraunces Tavern

Tontine Coffee House

Murray's Wharf

East River

Whitehall Slip (Ferries to Staten Island and Governors Island)

New York City Landmarks

fort and discovered the insult of an English flag nailed to the flagstaff. To make the insult worse, the English greased the flagstaff to prevent anyone from climbing it to remove the flag. A New York sailor by the name of John Van Arsdale put on a pair of iron cleats, climbed the flagstaff, and to the cheers of his compatriots tore down the English flag and replaced it with the Stars and Stripes.

Next stop on the list of historical landmarks is Trinity Church, an easy four blocks north on Broadway at the intersection with Wall Street. As you depart the fort to walk up Broadway, just before you come to the Bowling Green, off to your left and close to the Hudson River you will see an odd shaped flagstaff that looks strangely like a butter churn. Locals who meet friends for a variety of activities in this area laughingly tell everyone to meet them at "the butter churn."

On Evacuation Day, John Van Arsdale climbed the Fort George flagpole and replaced the English flag with the Stars and Stripes.

Trinity Church

Trinity Church, founded by the charter of King William III of England in 1697, is New York's oldest Episcopal Church. The church that you see before you is actually the second Trinity Church; the original having been destroyed by fire in 1776. This Trinity Church was finally completed just three years ago and carries on the long tradition of its predecessor as the church of New York's high society. This role was best expressed by Judge Thomas Jones in his memoirs: "Trinity enjoys the most influence, and greatest opulence. To this

Trinity Church is the tallest building in New York. Be sure to climb the spire for a wonderful view of the city.

Church, the Governor, the Lieutenant-Governor, most of his Majesties Council, many members of the General Assembly, all officers of the government, with a numerous train of rich and affluent merchants, and landlords belonged."[12]

Easily the tallest structure in the city, the church stands two hundred feet off the ground at the tip of its spire. If you care to make the climb to the top, 286 steps, you are rewarded with a spectacular 360-degree sweeping view of the city from the harbor all the way to the farms at the north end of Manhattan. High up here swings the bronze church bell, a gift of the bishop of London in 1711. When the first Trinity Church burned down in 1776, this bell was rescued from the ashes.

The church is capable of accommodating 350 parishioners in the pew boxes. These pew boxes have high wooden sides to keep everyone warm in the winter. Each pew box is assigned to a New York family, all of whom are quite wealthy and pay a substantial sum for the privilege of reserving a box. The closer the pew box is to the pulpit, the more expensive the annual rent; anywhere between 110 and 125 silver dollars.

The architectural highlights of the church are its spire and interior chapel. The red sandstone spire is ornately decorated by a series of small gargoyles scattered from top to bottom interspersed with small windows that illuminate its interior. The chapel is the largest in the city and is illuminated by two massive banks of windows on the east and west sides that are the largest in the city. The massive windows provide enough light so that the eight hanging candelabras, each holding one hundred candles, are rarely needed during daylight hours.

To find the next place on the tour, Federal Hall, exit the church's front door and walk directly east down Wall Street two blocks to Nassau Street.

Federal Hall

At the corner of Wall and Nassau Streets stands the imposing Federal Hall. First constructed in 1699, it was more recently renovated in 1788 by the French architect Pierre L'Enfant. For historians of the American Revolution, this monument is the site of the first presidential inauguration. On April 30, 1789, President George Washington stood on the front porch and swore his oath of office. Of equal if not greater importance to legal scholars, this is

One Neighborhood to Avoid

Not all of the city's cultural and historic sites are aesthetically pleasant experiences. One such place to avoid is a neighborhood called Five Points, the only place where the poorest can afford to live. Five Points is located at the intersection of five streets, hence its name, not far from the Collect Pond at the north end of the city and the Negro Burial Ground. Five Points is widely recognized as the worst slum in the city. Amid its beer breweries, smelly tanneries, bordellos, and tobacco manufacturers, is a maze of narrow alleys void of sunlight because of tall rickety tenement houses on either side. The alleys are little more than foul muddy lanes blocked by refuse, choked with pools of slime, and smelling of chemicals discharged by the tanneries and breweries.

This is a neighborhood where newly arrived foreigners and freed African slaves, all speaking a variety of languages, fight for survival in a city that can be a dangerous cultural mix. Most families pool their resources and crowd into single tenement houses with other equally destitute families. Often four or five single men working the night shift share beds in a single-room apartment with four or five other men working the day shift. Under such circumstances, gangs, theft, and violence are an unfortunate way of life.

also the place where the First Congress met and wrote the Bill of Rights.

Easy to locate because of its imposing size, Federal Hall stands a commanding fifty feet to the roof and another twenty-five above it to the top of the cupola. Along the south side is its most striking architectural feature, an immense stately outdoor balcony supported by four enormous white wood columns.

Take a walk around this wonderful example of Federalist architecture. Down each side visitors can see several large banks of windows that illuminate the many meeting rooms presently used by New York City's city council. When the president and the Congress moved to Philadelphia three years ago, Federal Hall became City Hall, the name now more commonly used. Inside, you are able to see many of the offices once used by the First Congress and the tables on which many drafts as well as the final Bill of Rights were penned.

From here, backtrack two blocks to Broadway, turn right, and proceed to Vesey Street, a brisk fifteen-minute walk, where you will catch sight of Saint Paul's Church.

New Yorkers stroll down Wall Street, past the grand columns of Federal Hall. Trinity Church is visible in the background.

Sunlight streams through the large windows of City Hall. If government meetings are not in session, visitors may tour the interior offices.

Saint Paul's Church

Built in 1766, Saint Paul's Church is George Washington's church. President Washington worshiped here for two years prior to the War of Independence, and following his inauguration as the nation's first president, he came here to be officially received by the grateful congregation. For history aficionados, this church is well worth the visit.

Saint Paul's is modeled after the English architect James Gibbs's well-known London church, Saint Martin-in-the-Fields. Several architects played a role in its overall completion, including Andrew Gautier, James Crommelin Lawrence, and Thomas McBean, a protégé of James Gibbs.

Saint Paul's is built of a very hard dense stone known as Manhattan schist that was quarried from the churchyard and of another hard stone known as brownstone. The west end of the building on Church Street supports the church's spire while the east end is designed as a carriage porch. It has classic details of imposing architecture, including the templelike Greek columns which hold up the enormous front porch. Above the front porch is a triangular inset pediment that holds an original American primitive handcarved oak statue of Saint Paul.

Under the Buttonwood Tree

In 1791 New York's financiers were eager to invest their money in honest companies. Two years earlier, public stocks were sold at a coffeehouse three times a week but, unfortunately, most of the stock bought and sold was controlled by a very small number of speculators who tricked others into buying overvalued stock. Between the contrived stock sales, dealers met under the branches of the buttonwood tree on Wall Street to trade stock legitimately.

By the end of the year, in need of a legitimate office to conduct business, they chartered the New York Stock Exchange Office on Wall Street. Unfortunately, the market collapsed and the public again lost confidence in the fledgling enterprise. On May 17 of last year, twenty-four brokers drew up the Buttonwood Agreement that laid the foundation for the fledgling stock market. At the beginning of this year, the volume of stock sales increased and a group of traders recognized the importance of establishing legitimate rules and regulations governing the sale of stock. To provide greater legitimacy for their business, they agreed to move to a new location in a rented room at the

Traders met outdoors on Wall Street before the new Stock Exchange headquarters were established.

Tontine Coffee House on the northwest corner of Wall and Water Streets, where members of the Stock Exchange continue to meet. The stock market has now stabilized.

Inside, hanging in the galleries, are fourteen original cut glass chandeliers. Below the east window is the first American monument dedicated to a Revolutionary soldier, General Richard Montgomery, who died at the Battle of Quebec. In the spire, should you choose to climb there, the largest bell is inscribed in Latin, "Mears London, Fecit 1779," meaning it was made by Mears (William Mears) in London in 1779. This bell was made from the same cast as was the Liberty Bell in Philadelphia.

During the British occupation in the Revolutionary War years, English generals Cornwallis and Howe attended services at Saint Paul's Church. After the war, on April 30, 1789, a special thanksgiving service was held in honor of President Washington's inauguration. For the two years during which New York was the nation's capital, Washington attended Saint Paul's making his personal pew of historical significance. Should you attend Sunday services, you will note that his pew remains vacant during services except on rare occasions when he is in town and he attends services.

When you exit Saint Paul's, make an immediate left turn on Broadway, walk three blocks north and turn left on Murray. As you look up, you will easily locate the spire on top of the cupola of Columbia College, your last stop on the tour. As you passed the New York Common, just off to the right as you departed Saint Paul's, the tall pole you saw is the Liberty Pole. New York patriots erected this pole on the Common as a symbol of resistance to the English Crown and it became one of the great rallying points for civil disobedience.

Columbia College

The cultural life of a major city is not complete without a major college. Fortunately for educated visitors

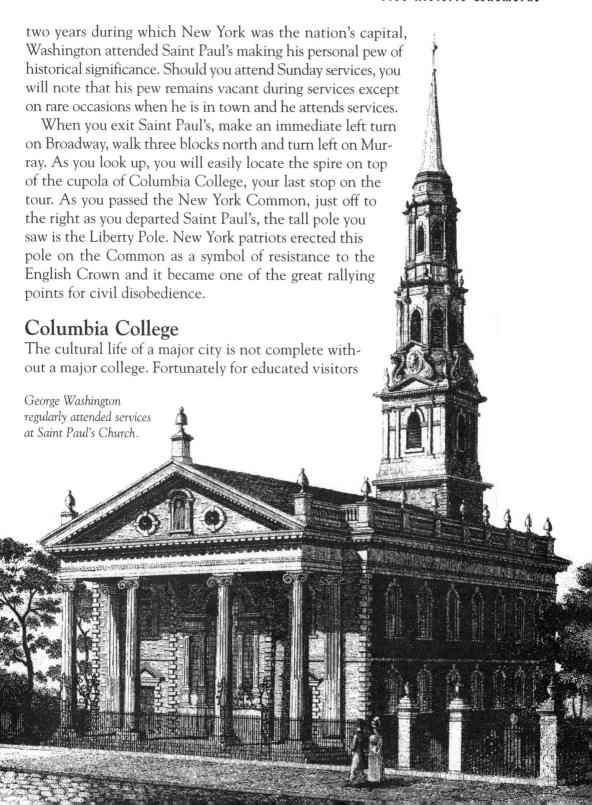

George Washington regularly attended services at Saint Paul's Church.

as well as historians, New York can proudly boast of Columbia College, located in the northwest corner of the city on Murray Street in between Chapel and Church Streets. A visit to this august institution of higher education will give you an opportunity to tour the facility, learn of its role in shaping the nation's democracy, and perhaps secure a place for your son in the next freshman class. At Columbia College, the future leaders of New York

receive an education designed, as an inscription here states, to, "Enlarge the Mind, improve the Understanding, polish the whole Man, and qualify them to support the brightest Characters in all the elevated stations in life."[13]

Columbia College was founded in 1754 as King's College by royal charter of King George II of England, but following the war the name was changed to Columbia College. It is the oldest institution of higher learning in the state of New York and the fifth oldest in the United States. In 1754 the sole teacher, Samuel Johnson, who was also the president of the college, taught eight students in the inaugural freshman class. One of the earliest goals of the college was to establish the first American medical school, and in 1767 that goal was realized.

The college is justifiably proud of its many alumni who played a role in the War of Independence and who later continued to serve the new nation. Among them is John Jay, the current chief justice of the Supreme Court; Alexander Hamilton, the current secretary of the Treasury; Gouverneur Morris, the author of the final draft of the Constitution; and Robert R. Livingston, a member of the five-man committee that drafted the Declaration of Independence.

Today the college has fourteen faculty members and 390 students. A tour of the college cannot fail to impress educated visitors because of the new main building completed just three years ago. This ele-

The Liberty Pole

One of the most identifiable symbols of independence from English rule is the Liberty Pole. This pole was initially an eighty-foot ship's mast set up by the Sons of Liberty and topped with a bronze weather vane inscribed with the word, *Liberty.* Set up on the New York Common, it was the rally point for patriotic activities aimed against the English.

When the pole was first erected in 1765, it became the unofficial assembly place for New York patriots whenever outrage against the English boiled over. Following a year of rebellious activity, English soldiers cut down the pole but a new one was defiantly erected the next year. Then, on August 11, 1766, the first blood of the fight for American liberty was spilled on the New York Common when citizens, outraged that it had for a third time been cut down, threw pieces of brick at the British troops who arrived to disperse them. In the ensuing skirmish, several Americans were bloodied in the fracas. By the time the British departed New York in 1776, six Liberty Poles had been erected.

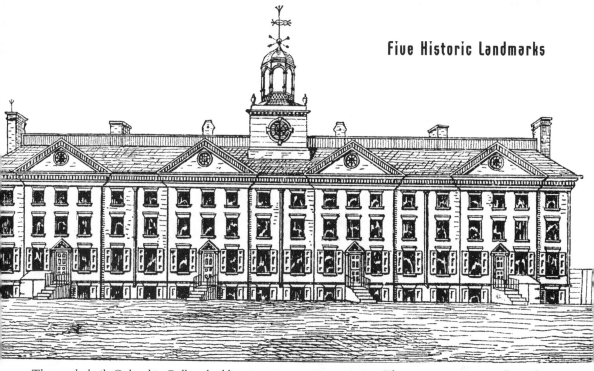

The newly built Columbia College building is an impressive structure. The entire campus is well worth a visit.

gant four-story building is easily identified from a distance by its twenty-foot cupola that sits on the roof in the middle of the rectangular building. This stone and concrete building is so large, 160 feet long, 62 feet wide, and 40 feet to the roof, that architects specified four separate entry doors. Not only is the building one of the largest in New York, it is also one of the more architecturally innovative. Above each of the four entry doors is a triangular cornice and in the center of each cornice is a round window. A quick walk around the building will lead visitors to two grassy fields where faculty occasionally hold classes on warm summer days.

Following a day of historical visits, a day touring some of the islands off the tip of New York might be a way to relax and take in some of New York's scenic marshes, mansions, wildlife, and rustic past. Although the city claims two dozen or more islands, the four closest are the most interesting and the most accessible.

Chapter 5

Island Tours

New York City is more than the lower tip of Manhattan Island. A part of New York exists less than a mile off the coast in the form of dozens of islands, both large and small. Each has its own personality, its own history, and each is only a short ferryboat ride away. Walk down to the docks at the lower tip of the city to locate the Staten Island Ferry dock where boats for most islands depart on a regular basis. For visitors with only a few days to become acquainted with New York, consider touring Governors, Bedloe's, Gibbet, Staten, and Long Islands.

Giovanni da Verrazano

Governors Island

Just half a mile off the tip of Manhattan, Governors Island is 175 acres of fascinating history, old colonial estates, and farmland. For the price of a three-cent ticket, vacationers are rowed across the narrow strait on a boat operated by Captain John Hillyer, the registered owner of the ferry between New York and the island.

The first European to see Governors Island was Verrazano who changed the name from its original Indian name of Pagganck to the Dutch name Nooten Eylandt or Nutten Island. According to local historians, in June 1637 the Dutch bought the island from the Manhattan Indians for what is believed to have been two iron ax heads, a string of glass beads, and a handful of nails, none of which had ever been seen by the Indians. The name was again changed to Governors Island in 1698 when it became the dedicated home for English colonial governors.

Still standing and of interest is the governor's mansion. Built in 1703 by Governor Cornbury, it overlooks Buttermilk

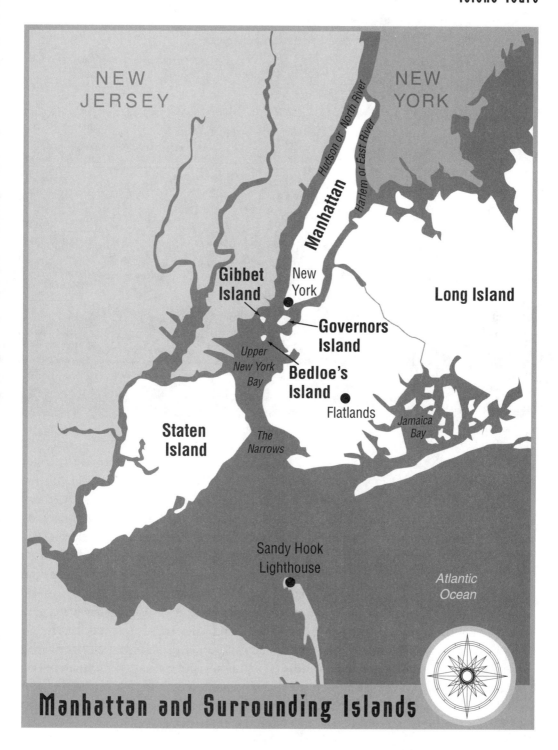

Manhattan and Surrounding Islands

A trip to Bedloe's Island will cost four cents by ferry, but it is well worth the fare. From shore, visitors can enjoy a fine view of the city.

Channel that separates Governors Island from Long Island. Since the mansion was intended to be the governor's mansion as well as his place of office, the mansion includes his personal living quarters in addition to offices and conference rooms. The mansion was continuously occupied until June 7, 1775, when a contingent of General Washington's troops under the command of General Putnam drove the governor and his staff from the island. Not much later, however, in September 1776, the English recaptured the island and held it until the end of the war.

Today the island is under the control of New York State governor George Clinton and there is much discussion as to its future. The governor, who has authority over the island, recently authorized a lease for the construction of a race track as well as a fancy summer resort. A walk around the island's beautiful gardens and trees argues for making the island a public park for the city's growing population but military personnel, led by Supreme Court justice John Jay, believe a fort defending New York Harbor would be the better decision.

Bedloe's Island

One mile to the immediate west of Governors Island is the diminutive Bedloe's Island. Although very small, merely forty acres, it has had a long and interesting history. The Indians originally called it Minnissais, meaning Lesser Island, until it was acquired by the English. At that time, in 1667, the governor of New York gave the island to Captain Robert Needham who turned right around the very next day and sold it to Isaak Bedloe.

For years the island was of little interest to anyone until 1738 when a smallpox epidemic struck the city and the island was established as the city's first quarantine station. All ships arriving from islands within the West Indies, the origin of the disease, were first ordered to anchor at Bedloe's Island so doctors could row out to the boats and inspect the passengers and crew. Only then could they proceed into New York City. In 1746 Archibald Kennedy bought the island for the sum of three hundred dollars for use as a summer home. During his ownership, New York ordered the erection of a beacon that could be ignited to signal New Jersey, Connecticut, and New York of the approach of an enemy. When the English occupied New York, they seized Bedloe's Island and used it as a refuge for English sympathizers. Objecting to this use, New York patriots managed to set fire to many of the buildings on the island.

Governor George Clinton

Today the small but picturesque island is a popular weekend escape from the noise, smells, and congestion of the city. A ferryboat ride of four cents is a worthwhile cost to come here for the day to hike the island and enjoy lunch. From here, one has one of the best possible views of the New York skyline, the coasts of Governors Island and Staten Island to the south, as well as a view of all incoming ships from the Atlantic.

Standing on the north point of the island, tourists can see the equally small Gibbet Island just a short boat ride to the north. Although the island is owned by Samuel Ellis, the name Ellis Island has not taken hold among New Yorkers. The short boat ride makes the visit easy and worthwhile.

Gibbet Island

During high tide, Gibbet Island can scarcely be seen above the rising waters. Because of its low profile in the water, it supports the richest assortment of wildlife in the New York area. In fact, the first two names for the island were animal names. The local Indian tribes called it Kioshk, or Gull Island, and later, when the Dutch acquired it, they called it Oyster Island, a reference to its rich and abundant oyster beds. Also unusual about the island is its shape. It has the appearance of a rectangle with a long narrow notch cut into one side that provides a perfect port for boats to enter and tie up.

After being developed for its rich oyster beds, the island became a favorite haunt for Anderson, the pirate who hid here and attacked small ships as they departed the harbor heavily laden with cargo. But in 1765 the island was again renamed, this time after the gibbet, an upright post with a crosspiece forming a T-shaped structure used for hanging criminals. Anderson was finally caught that year, hanged, and because of his legendary reputation for daring attacks on shipping, the city voted to rename the island Gibbet Island after the instrument of his execution. Eventually, on January 20, 1785, wealthy merchant Samuel Ellis purchased the property and he still owns it today.

A pirate's hanging inspired the name for Gibbet Island.

New Yorkers come here to relax, fish, dig clams along the beach, pick bird eggs from the thick marshes for their breakfasts, and fish for the plentiful and profitable shad that swim through the narrow channels of the bay. The waters around the island are so rich with edible sea life that when Ellis purchased the island, rumors circulated that he offered to purchase it with "A few barrels of excellent fat shad . . . and a few thousand red herring of his own curing [seasoning]."[14]

In addition to the fishing and hunting for shellfish, this small island is also a great place to wander the cannon batteries placed here by the English to defend New York Harbor. The brick and rock escarpments that you see were built to protect the cannoneers from the balls fired from enemy ships. Installed below the low escarpment are the cannons, which have not yet been removed because of continuing fear that the English may again return in an attempt to retake New York. The cannons are set low yet just high enough for their barrels to extend above the escarpment to fire out to sea. These cannons fire the heavy sixty-four-pound balls capable of snapping the masts of enemy ships, raking their decks with destruction, and when perfectly aimed at the water line, inflicting sufficient damage to flood and slow the ship and eventually sink it.

Staten Island

Located five miles off the tip of Manhattan, Staten Island is the second largest of the islands on the recommended tour. Its sixty square miles take the shape of an elongated diamond. As was the case with all of the land in this region, the early inhabitants were the Lenape who referred to the island as Eghquaons. Its present name came from the Dutch who named the island Staten Eylandt, meaning in Dutch, "States Island." At the north point is where the freshwater of the Hudson River blends with the saltwater of the Atlantic Ocean.

It was not until 1670 that the island was purchased from the local Indians, after which they departed to make room for a few hundred farmers and a few dozen scattered wealthy estate owners. During the war, Staten Island played a major role as the place where English soldiers, at one time thirty thousand of them—ten times the island's population—mustered before engaging in battle. Eventually, as was the case with the rest of New York, the English withdrew in 1783.

Today, as you wander the island on horseback or by carriage, you see saltwater marshes filled with every imaginable type of sea and migratory bird such as herons, egrets, snow geese, ducks, and gulls. The birds share the marshes with fiddler crabs, box turtles, and the harmless black racer snake. Nearby are many small picturesque fishing villages, a few small shipping ports, and the scenic Dutch-designed windmills used to mill local grain into flour and to cut lumber. Farther inland you pass by small farms tilled by teams of oxen and draft horses within thick stands of pitch pine forests that are milled for lumber at the local sawmills.

Toward the center of the island, at the intersection of Victory Boulevard and Richmond Avenue, is the Bull's Head Tavern. Just before the war this was a favorite gathering place of Tories, the turncoat Americans who supported the English and hoped that they would win the war. Right next door happens to be the Asbury Methodist Church

Staten Island's landscape is dotted with quaint Dutch windmills.

The Taylor Sawmill on Staten Island

Of all of the machinery driven by waterwheels here in the New York area, the sawmill is the most common. Most mills are owned and operated by farmers of above average means who run them seasonally as water levels and the demands of their farmwork permit. They serve entire neighborhoods due to the expense of transporting high-weight but low-value lumber any great distance over land. One of the best is the Taylor mill that can be found on Staten Island and if you go there, the miller will gladly give you a tour.

The Taylor sawmill, like most in the New York area, consists of a straight saw blade, six feet long and tightly bolted to a rectangular wooden frame called a "sash." The saw sash is in turn connected to a waterwheel by way of a wooden arm called a "sweep" or "pitman arm" that is turned by water cascading over a dam onto the waterwheel. The turning motion of the waterwheel is converted to the up-and-down motion of the saw blade by the pitman arm. As the waterwheel turns, power from the saw sash is used to turn a large gear, called a "rag wheel." This in turn moves the carriage which the log rests on, pulling the log through the saw. The saw cuts into the log on its downstroke, and then the log moves forward on the upstroke; about three-eighths of an inch each time. After one board is sawed off on one side of the log, the log carriage is run back to the other end of the mill, the log moved over, and another board cut. This process is repeated until the whole log has been sawed into lumber. Often a sawyer will square up two sides of a log first and then turn the log ninety degrees so that the flat sides are on the top and bottom. Using this technique, all the sawed boards will have razor-sharp straight edges.

Sawmill owners charge local farmers by the board foot—one foot by one foot by one inch—to saw their logs into boards, planks, and timbers. In one day the Taylor sawmill can cut as much lumber as two men working by hand for one week. The capacity of this sawmill is limited to logs ten feet in length and twenty-eight inches in diameter and it operates at about sixty strokes per minute.

A Staten Island farmer hauls logs to the local sawmill.

Staten Island's Bulls Head Tavern can provide food for a picnic. From high on the island's hill, the views of Manhattan and Upper New York Bay are stunning.

and if you wander around the back, you come across a small graveyard where you will find the headstone of a local character by the name of Ichabod Crane, a local schoolteacher known for looking for ghosts in the woods and making up charms to ward off evil spirits.

Before departing, glance off to the southeast on a clear day and spot the lighthouse on the Sandy Hook Peninsula, the only lighthouse in the New York waters.

Sandy Hook Lighthouse

New York Harbor has only one lighthouse on the Sandy Hook Peninsula to the southwest of the city. Only the fifth built in America, it sits five hundred feet from the shoreline. The structure is an octagonal tower built from local rubble covered with mortar. The 103-foot-tall tower has a diameter of 29 feet at the base and the lantern house at the top of the light is made of iron with a copper-clad roof. On June 11, 1764, the forty-eight whale oil lamps were lit for the first time to guide fishermen, mariners, and travelers passing in and out of New York Harbor. The lamps installed in the crown are of copper encased in a lantern of ordinary glass. The keeper, whose principal responsibility is to trim the wicks and light the lamps, lives in the stone house beside the tower.

The Sandy Hook lighthouse has guided ships into New York harbor for decades.

Long Island

The largest island off the southeastern tip of New York is Long Island. Aptly named to describe the island's 118-mile length by 20-mile width, this rural island is inhabited by a few farmers, ranchers, fishermen, and a handful of Indians scattered along the northern tip.

Today's attractions on the island are primarily its rural environment. This is a favorite place for New Yorkers who enjoy several days of hunting and fishing or for day trips along the East River to picnic, pick blueberries, and attend thoroughbred horse racing.

One unusual activity of interest to many architects and historians is a visit to the one of the first original Dutch colonial farmhouses at New Amersfoort, known today as the town of Flatlands. The home was built around 1652 by Pieter Claesen, who arrived in America in 1637 as an illiterate indentured servant. The house that you see before you today reflects renovations carried out around 1740 although much of the original house can still be seen.

Many of the high points of architectural interest of the fourteen-hundred-square-foot house are viewable from the outside. The structure is a one-and-a-half-story home with shingled walls and wide overhanging eaves; an attic is above half of the house. Three brick chimneys extend above the pitched shingled roof, and ample windows, an extravagant expense in the 1600s, illuminate the interior. If you wander the

The shingles and wide eaves of the old Claesen farmhouse make it one of the best examples of Dutch colonial architecture found on Long Island.

exterior, you will find three entry doors; private entries for each of the three interior rooms.

Inside, the interior space is divided into three long and narrow separate rooms, each of which runs the length of the house. One is the kitchen and the other two are sleeping rooms, called chamber rooms. The ceilings are about nine feet tall; high by the standards of the time. One room has a hole in the ceiling that leads to the attic, which is

69

Jamaica Bay

Just a short six-mile ride across the East River to Long Island, vacationers will find an unusually beautiful collection of small islands encapsulated within a large cove named Jamaica Bay. Hidden and protected from the ravages of the harsh Atlantic Ocean, Jamaica Bay provides a placid and quiet retreat from the noise, smell, and congestion of New York City.

For New Yorkers, the dozens of islands within the bay are hideaways for those longing to experience the simple pleasures of hunting and fishing. It does not really matter which island you choose to visit—Barren, Big Egg, Ruffle Bar, Bergen, or Mill—each presents the same opportunities for a week of recreation and relaxation.

The warm summer breezes attract many vacationers to the islands accessed by small private ferryboats that shuttle visitors. Unlike the larger ferryboats that ply the waters just off the lower tip of Manhattan, these small boats depart only when they are full; be prepared for a long wait. Once tourists reach their inns they will find time to dig for clams and oysters, fish for a variety of small local catch, or just sit in the sun.

One of the most colorful and picturesque times of the year to visit the bay's islands occurs in the spring when millions of migrating birds arrive in the bay to feed before continuing farther north for the summer. Sightseers will find the noise deafening as enormous flocks of heron, swan, egrets, snow geese, and duck circle the bay before landing to feed and rest. For a month or so, this colorful collection of fowl snack on billions of insects, small horseshoe crabs, newly hatched fry, and the floating eggs of local fish. Hunters will find ample opportunities to hunt these birds. Favorites among the local folks for dinner are the ducks and snow geese.

the slaves' quarters. One of the additions of 1740 is the underground basement called the root cellar where vegetables, fruits, and cider are stored to keep everything cool. It is called a root cellar because most of the vegetables such as potatoes, onions, leeks, and yams are from the root family.

Following a day or two of energetic tromping around New York's rural islands, a few days of casual entertainment closer to the city will bring some welcome rest.

Chapter 6

Casual Entertainment

New York has a lot to offer in the way of sports, both spectator and participatory, public events that raise money for a variety of civic causes, and a few activities that can only be found in New York.

America's Gambling Den

For those with a penchant for gambling, New York has more opportunities than Boston and Philadelphia combined. Legalized gambling can be found at shuffleboard clubs, billiard tables in some of the city's more expensive taverns, horse-racing tracks, card parlors, bare-knuckle boxing matches, cock fights, and city-controlled lotteries. Without a doubt, New York is America's "gambling den."

Lotteries controlled by the city have been popular in New York for more than one hundred years. Tickets can be pur-chased at tobacco shops and must be held until the official drawing of the winning number. Each ticket has a unique number and whoever holds the winning ticket is entitled to the entire pool of lottery money minus the 15 percent that goes into the city's coffers. Each ticket has printed on it this explanation of the rules: "The Possessor of this Ticket, if drawn a Prize, shall by Virtue of a Law of this State, be entitled to the Prize so drawn, sub-ject to Fifteen Percent de-duction."[15] In the past, New York has used lottery pro-ceeds to subsidize the building of Sandy Hook Lighthouse, building programs on the campus of Columbia College, repairs to city buildings, and as public assistance for destitute women and children.

Horse Racing

For those who would enjoy a day at the races, a short boat ride across the East River to Long Island and the Newmarket track at the city of Salisbury Plain is the place to go. This is one of the few organized places of entertainment enjoyed equally by both men and women.

Fortuitously for horse-racing aficionados, Salisbury Plain is home to expansive lush grassy fields ideally suited to racing. Other established tracks include Newmarket II, Washington, Ascot Heath (where the British raced during the Revolution), and Beaver Pond. In 1750 racing's elite met at Newmarket to form the Jockey Club that continues to organize horse races and to exercise control over races with a complex set of rules to ensure fair and safe racing.

The configuration of the track is a two-mile oval run over a thick mat of grass.

Lotteries, billiards, and other games of chance await those visitors with a fondness for gambling.

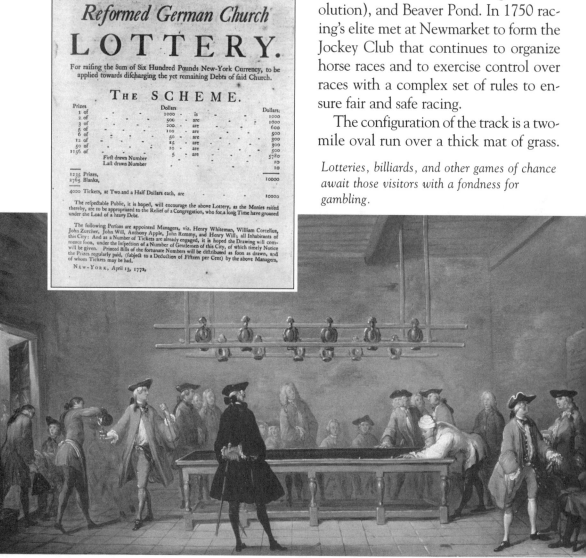

THE

Reformed German Church

LOTTERY.

For raising the Sum of Six Hundred Pounds New-York Currency, to be applied towards discharging the yet remaining Debts of said Church.

THE SCHEME.

Prizes		Dollars				Dollars
1 of		1000	is			1000
2 of		500	are			1000
3 of		200	are			600
5 of		100	are			500
6 of		50	are			300
12 of		25	are			300
50 of		10	are			500
1156 of		5	are			5780
	First drawn Number					10
	Last drawn Number					10
1235 Prizes,						
2765 Blanks,						10000
4000 Tickets, at Two and a Half Dollars each, are						10000

The respectable Public, it is hoped, will encourage the above Lottery, as the Monies raised thereby, are to be appropriated to the Relief of a Congregation, who for a long Time have groaned under the Load of a heavy Debt.

The following Persons are appointed Managers, viz. Henry Whiteman, William Corcelius, John Zurcher, John Will, Anthony Apple, John Remmy, and Henry Will, all Inhabitants of this City: And as a Number of Tickets are already engaged, it is hoped the Drawing will commence soon, under the Inspection of a Number of Gentlemen of this City, of which timely Notice will be given. Printed Bills of the fortunate Numbers will be distributed as soon as drawn, and the Prizes regularly paid, (subject to a Deduction of Fifteen per Cent) by the above Managers, of whom Tickets may be had.

New-York, April 13, 1772.

Seating is not provided. Everyone must be prepared to stand or bring their own chairs. Prior to the start of the races, gentlemen may inspect the horses and place their wagers; an important ingredient that enhances the excitement of the day. The race day is a lengthy affair lasting most of the day, so bring a lunch to enjoy between the races.

The layout of the track has room for only twenty horses to run safely for the first-place prize but far more than twenty horses show up each race day. To pare the number down, several heats are run until the best twenty are decided. The final race begins late in the afternoon when a rope restraining all horses is dropped and they are off. The race is a blur of horses and flying tufts of grass. The horses pound down the turf in a dash. Bettors strain to keep the pack in sight as they round each turn of the oval. The fastest horses are ridden by professional riders called jockeys who are lightweight men trained in horse-racing tactics. The first horse to cross the finish line is declared the winner as long as the horse remained within the course boundaries, the jockey did not fall off, and the winning jockey did not illegally obstruct other horses, or assault rival riders with his whip.

Upon the completion of the Newmarket race, a dignitary announces the winner and presents a silver cup. This official cup is awarded twice a year at special races in the spring and in the fall. During the presentation, the official explains that the reason for the trophy is "Not so

A Fourteen-Mile Drive

One of the most enjoyable ways to entertain oneself in New York is to experience the fourteen-mile ride around Manhattan. An all-day trip by rented carriage departs at the Boston Post Road in eastern Lower Manhattan and carries vacationers as far north as Harlem, traveling through the pleasant green countryside and then back down to the city.

One of the more picturesque areas the drive passes through is Grin'wich, sometimes spelled Greenwich. Although quite marshy and remote, it is a pastoral region spotted with small farms and occasional manors built by wealthy New York businessmen as summer retreats for their families. Even in the winter, rented carriages will still make the trip on iron rails that convert the carriages into sleighs. Winter is a favorite time for loads of young people to ride out into the country to have dinner and then dance at one of the rural taverns. Governor John Drayton of South Carolina made this same fourteen-mile ride and according to Susan Elizabeth Lyman in her book *The Story of New York: An Informal History of the City,* he proclaimed, "The rides in the neighborhood of the city are for miles beautiful. Every elevation of ground, presenting some handsome country vista—with what pleasure I have often viewed them."

much for the divertisement of youth as for encouraging the bettering of the breed of horses, which through great neglect [because of the war] had been impaired."[16]

Trainers and jockeys prepare their horses for a race. For a perfect day at the racetrack, spectators should bring chairs, lunch, and plenty of money for wagering.

Fox Hunting

If fox hunting is of interest to visiting gentlemen, the two men to find when you arrive are James de Lancey and Lewis Morris. They hold a weekly fox hunt on the outskirts of the city, either in an area across the East River on Long Island or north of the city in the farming region of Harlem. Wherever the fox is hunted, these two gentlemen provide the fox and the hounds; you must provide your own horse. To find out where the hunt will take place, ride over to either the King's Head or Cato's Taverns where the proprietors advertise the hunt with broadsides posted above the door.

At a specified time and place, the master of the hunt assembles all involved in the hunt. It is his responsibility to explain all rules regarding the hunt to avoid injury to riders and hounds. The hounds, usually between eight and ten beagles or Irish hounds are controlled by the terryman who determines when they are released and when retrieved. The third official to play a pivotal role in the hunt is the fox-finder, who scouts the countryside until he finds a fox hiding in a burrow or under a log.

Once a fox is located, the fox-finder signals the master of the hunt and the terryman to close in. When the hounds are about one hundred yards from the fox and have picked up his scent, they begin a relentless yelping as they strain at the leashes to pursue the fox. With a nod of the master's head, the terryman unleashes the hounds and as soon as the fox sees them coming, he takes off running. Following close behind the hounds are the huntsmen on their horses.

The fox instinctively runs toward creeks, fences, thick brush, and rocky outcroppings to escape the hounds. The real skill and thrill of the hunt is for the riders to stay on their mounts as they vault low fences, splash across streams, and crash through rough thickets in pursuit of the hounds and the fox. The hunt ends when the hounds either catch the fox or force it into a burrow or up a tree. If the hounds catch the fox, the master of the hunt allows them to tear it to shreds and eat it. If, on the other hand, the fox is treed or stuck in a burrow, the master of the hunt may spare its life.

At that moment, the hunt is over and the socializing begins. As exhilarating and romantic as the chase might be, it is the party that follows that draws most participants. All riders reassemble at a tavern for a toast of ale, a proper banquet, and the sharing of stories of each rider's spills and triumphal displays of cuts and bruises.

Gentlemen will enjoy the thrill of the foxhunt, as well as the banquet after the chase, where hunters share their exploits with each other.

Lawn bowling was popular with the early Dutch settlers. Interested visitors can find a game to join at the public bowling green near Fort George.

Lawn Bowling

A slower and more civilized form of entertainment than fox hunting can be found at the foot of Broadway and Beaver Streets, down by Fort George on the Battery. This home to lawn bowling enthusiasts is called New York's Bowling Green. This small triangular park was laid out as a public bowling green in 1733 for the unusual price of one peppercorn per member. This strange price was set many years ago when scarce spices were often used in place of money.

The park is surrounded by a wrought iron fence—the same one erected in 1771. If the fence looks a bit odd, it is because the top of each twelfth spike looks as if something has been twisted off of it; and it has. In July 1776, after the Declaration of Independence was declared, a triumphant mob of patriots ripped the bronze crows, which to them symbolized the English monarchy, off the tops of the spikes.

Within the elegant low fence is the actual bowling green. The object of the game is to win points by rolling one's black wood balls closest to a small white ball called the "jack." The jack may be anywhere on the green as long as it is between seventy-five and one hundred feet away from the bowling end line. The skill, some say the art, is to roll one's set of balls as close to the jack as possible even when an opponent may have positioned his balls to intentionally block the jack. When all players have rolled all of their balls, the winner is determined as the player with the most balls closest to the jack.

Lawn Bowling Strategy

Strategy plays a role in lawn bowling. Choosing the right size and weight ball is just as important as whether the balls are rolled underhand or sidearm. Sometimes they are bowled hard and straight to knock away guard balls, but at other times soft to get it right next to the jack. Often, if the green is littered with many balls, a good player is able to place a slight curve on the ball causing it to sweep past the guard balls and stop next to the jack. On the average bowling green, a good bowler can achieve about six feet of curve for every one hundred feet of distance.

Which type of delivery a bowler chooses is dependent on the position of other balls already in play. It is also determined by the condition of the bowling green and its own peculiarities such as the height and dampness of the grass. It is also important to remember that the jack may move during the game when struck by the other balls, often dramatically changing the outcome of the game with the very last ball bowled.

Public Pistol Duels

Public duels also attract large crowds of spectators. Although many consider the popularity of watching duels a perverse form of entertainment, they nonetheless attract large crowds when word about one gets out. Crowds of more than one thousand have been known to gather to take in the drama of two men shooting at each other.

Ever since dueling was introduced to America by the English and French, dozens of New York men have died or have been wounded defending their honor or the honor of a family member. When pistol duels are arranged, they typically take place on a Sunday morning at a field known as the dueling ground in Weehawken just across the East River. This location is a long narrow glen along a footpath lined with trees where throngs of spectators take macabre delight in witnessing the spectacle.

Most duels are triggered by an exchange of insulting remarks by men having drunk too much ale. When neither man is willing to apologize the next day, a challenge is offered. Few men presented with such a challenge refuse it for fear of being publicly ridiculed as a coward. Once a day, place, and time is set, the two combatants meet, usually at Weehawken, each with one supporter known as his "second." Under most circumstances, the rules that apply to the duel are those contained within the Code Duello that specifies precisely how the duel must be conducted: the type of pistol, the distance between the combatants, and the number of shots or wounds required for satisfaction of honor. Most pistol duels are decided on a single exchange of shots or the first ball that draws blood; rarely is either duelist killed.

A duel begins when the two adversaries arrive and review the rules. Then each man retires to consult with his second, to load his pistol—usually a smooth-bore flintlock with a half-inch ball—and to decide whether to offer or to request an apology before stepping to the middle of the dueling ground. When an apology seems unlikely, both men step to the fore.

Set back to back, each man, holding his loaded pistol in the vertical position to prevent the powder and ball from falling out of the barrel, takes one pace

Visitors may travel to the dueling grounds at Weehawken, New Jersey, with an easy ferry ride from New York, but the sport is not for the squeamish.

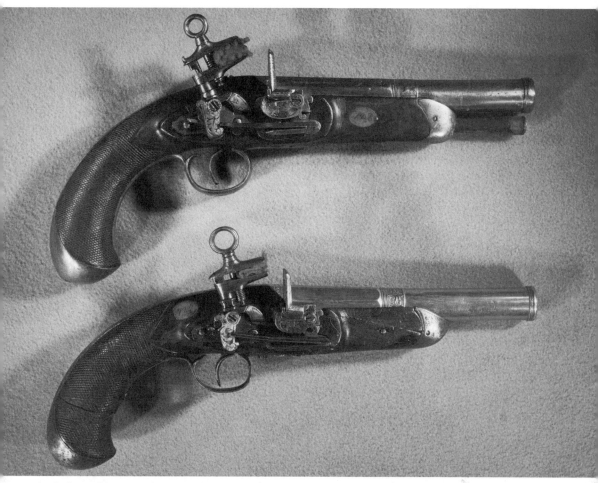

Flintlock pistols are popular with experienced duelists. The half-inch balls used as ammunition typically do not result in mortal wounds.

after another as each is called out by one of the seconds. As the distance between the two men increases with each step, and the final one is called—between ten and thirty paces—each man levels his arm and turns to face his adversary. A trained duelist exposes only his right side to his opponent, keeping his stomach drawn in and his right arm shielding as much of his chest as possible.

Each then fires his pistol. Sometimes both pistols misfire or both men miss with their shots. In either case, the duel is over and each opponent goes home having preserved his honor without a scratch. The most likely outcome is for one man to be wounded, which according to the Code Duello, ends the duel. "Any wound sufficient to agitate the nerves and necessarily make the hand shake must end the

The Huckleberry Frolic

An event visitors will not want to miss, especially those traveling with children, is the annual carnival called the Huckleberry Frolic. Each June, on the second Sunday of the month, families pack their picnic baskets, load their wagons and carriages, and travel across the East River to Long Island. The frolic is always a fun-filled day featuring a variety of athletic events, horse and mule races, comedians, fire-eaters, wild beasts, and gymnasts. Look for a steady stream of carriages and horses leading north to a broad valley large enough to accommodate the gathering, and follow them.

The Huckleberry Frolic is our annual "Day in the Country." Celebrating the beginning of summer, the annual event is usually a warm and sunny day. This is a time for children and parents to relax, chat with family members, gossip, talk about politics, and reestablish friendships following the long winter and busy spring.

Highest on the list for children, especially the boys, is a variety of athletic events. Footraces are organized into age categories for one-hundred- and four-hundred-yard races. A great ship's rope is brought from the docks to use in the annual tug-of-war that pits fifty city boys living on Manhattan against fifty farm boys living on Long Island. For some of the older boys, arm-wrestling contests are popular along with fence jumping and bow-and-arrow shooting contests.

Wandering through the picnic area is a variety of strolling entertainers popular with small children. Favorites are impromptu puppet shows, fire-eaters who ignite some sort of flammable substance and extinguish it by placing it in their mouths, men with bears on chains that perform tricks, men with long whips capable of snapping handkerchiefs out of a person's outstretched hand, and a colorful collection of jugglers and clowns.

business for that day."[17] Only on rare occasions does one man fall and die from a wound. Whatever the outcome, the Code Duello requires each man to remain calm under fire and to behave in a civil and courteous manner.

Far from the dueling ground, the turf of the race track, or the countryside of the fox hunt, Lower Manhattan attracts a different type of entertainment and a different type of New Yorker. In keeping with the great traditions of cosmopolitan centers such as London and Paris, sophisticated and educated citizens flock to attend the city's impressive array of cultural attractions.

Chapter 7

Cultural New York

When the Englishman John Lambert passed through New York last year, he highlighted the mile long stretch of Broadway from the Bowling Green north to the Common that he described as having: "Large commodious shops of every description . . . book stores, print-shops, music-shops, jewelers, and silversmiths; theaters, music halls, hatters, linen-drapers, milliners, pastry-cooks, coach makers, hotels, and coffeehouses; all for the pleasure of the cultured upper-class."[18]

Look to New York for the finest books, music, and theater.

This ward is the cultural heart of New York City. This area also happens to be the neighborhood for the wealthiest of the wealthy; successful merchants, lawyers, doctors, and maritime brokers live side by side in rows of elegant townhouses. To satisfy all of their cultural needs, cosmopolitan visitors touring New York will find an amazing variety and richness in the city's cultural offerings in spite of the recent war. The end of the war ushered in a new cultural and intellectual era providing New Yorkers with museums, elegant private social clubs, theaters, bookstores, and a throng of literary clubs such as the Calliopean Society, the Belles Lettres Club, and the Society for Promoting Useful Knowledge.

First on the cultural tour is the Tammany Museum, the largest and most eclectic museum in America. Londoners and Parisians, who have access to older and better established museums at home, will nonetheless find the museum's offerings unusual, educational, and uniquely American.

Broadway is the main thoroughfare in New York City. From the Bowling Green to the Common, the avenue is lined with fine homes, shops, theaters, and clubs.

The Tammany Museum

At the intersection of Nassau and Wall Streets, museumgoers will locate New York's Tammany Museum. This museum is just one more reason why New Yorkers think the city is the best in America; no other city can lay claim to having its own museum.

The first exhibit that visitors encounter, for which the museum was initially built, is its collection of Indian artifacts. That this collection should be the first is appropriate because the museum takes its name from the Indian chief Tammany who lived in the seventeenth century. He was chief of the Delaware tribe and according to one account, was the first Indian to welcome William Penn to this country in 1681.

The collection begins with grinding stones used to mill corn into flour. These stones have the shape of narrow deep bowls worn down by the friction of stone pestles used to grind the corn. Next is the exhibit of birchbarks, canoes commonly used by the local New York tribes, followed by deerskin clothing and an impressive array of wampum and weaponry such as spears, bows, and arrows.

Next is a collection of both live and taxidermied animals donated by Gardiner Baker. This collection of natural history can be enjoyed by people of all ages. The favorite live animal in the exhibit is a mountain lion, the favorite bizarre animal exhibit includes a fetus of an orangutan, and the largest animal exhibit is the twenty-two-foot-long pair of jawbones from a whale harpooned off the coast of Nantucket Island not far from Boston.

The final exhibit, also donated by Baker, is a collection of modern me- chanical devices primarily used on farms. This exhibit displays modern plows, threshing machines, the latest horse har- nesses and oxen yolks, and hand-swung sickles that cut stalks of grain and catch them in a cradle attached to the handle so they can be laid in a straight line for ease of later collection.

 # Public Schools

By the mid–eighteenth century, merchants, traders, and other classes of business leaders in New York recognized that the fi- nancial and cultural future of the city would rest on the shoulders of the literate. By the late 1780s there were half a dozen charity schools established for the poor as well a dozen private schools supported by tuition paid by the students' families.

Only seven years ago, the first school for freed Negroes, named the African Free School, was formed by the Manumission So- ciety. The school is located in a one-room building on Cliff Street. This school is the only place where boys can learn to read and write as well as learn everyday values and disci- pline. In order to be admitted to the school the boys must promise to remain sober, avoid associating with en- slaved blacks, and to live clean lives.

A schoolmaster instructs his young pupils.

The Theater

New Yorkers pride themselves in having the most active theater in America. Boston and Philadelphia combined cannot compete with what New York can offer. Any week that out-of-town guests choose to visit will be a week filled with theatrical offerings. The best way to find out about this week's theater bill is either to consult one of New York's newspapers that run advertisements for plays or to keep an eye peeled for broadsides posted on walls and buildings in the theater district on lower Broadway.

The one theater most likely to provide the highest quality productions is the John Street Theater on John Street just east of Broadway. When packed with patrons (and it usually is sold out), the theater accommodates 1,158 ticket holders. Gallery seats are four shillings, seats near the orchestra pit are six shillings, and the six tiers of boxes, each of which seats six people, are available to season ticket holders for only eight shillings per seat. Whichever tickets you purchase, no spectator is further than eighty feet from front stage and every word spoken by the actors and actresses can easily be heard.

Thus far this season the John Street Theater actors have performed several plays including Shakespeare's *Merchant of Venice*, *The King and the Miller of Mansfield*, by Robert Dodsley, and the French playwright Molière's *Tartuffe*.

Because of the popularity of the theater, the parking of carriages creates severe congestion on the street. When you arrive and step down from your carriage, please be sure that you instruct your coachman to properly tie up the horses according to the instructions on the broadside advertising the play. It requests all coachmen to "take up and set down with their horses heads toward the East-River."[19] If everyone follows these in-

 Broadsides

The culture and history of New York has been greatly enriched by the city's long tradition of posting broadsides. Broadsides are the most often used form of advertising in New York for theater, music, art exhibits, and political comment. These single large sheets of printed paper are tacked up on the sides of buildings, fences, public taverns, trees, on the sides of warehouses, inside coffeehouses, and a thousand other places.

For many years broadsides have been printed by small and often "underground" printers as an inexpensive way to express contentious and unconventional points of view. Before and during the war, broadsides were posted late at night recommending a variety of ways for New Yorkers to take part in acts of civil disobedience against the Crown.

The broadside read by the most citizens was the Declaration of Independence, but the one that had the greatest impact on the War of Independence was the one announcing the battle at Concord and Lexington on April 19, 1775. After those were posted, New Yorkers stormed down to the docks where English ships were unloaded of their cargo including 550 muskets stolen by patriots.

structions, the congestion can be lessened. The doors open at 5:00 P.M. and the curtain rises promptly at 6:15 P.M.

For those who prefer musicals to Shakespeare or Molière, a short walk over to the New Theater on Nassau Street will provide a gold mine of musical entertainment. Now that the war is over, touring companies are arriving from Europe and from other American cities to perform favorites such as John Gay's *Beggar's Opera* and Benjamin Carr's musical comedy, *The Archers of Switzerland*.

Classical Music

As is the case with theatrical productions, New York is also the classical music capital of America. Classical music has played a role in the city's abounding cultural life since its settlement. For the first hundred years or so, the favored place to hear classical music was Trinity Church because of its size and its beautifully handcrafted organ imported from Bavaria, Germany. With the construction of the New Theater on Nassau Street, however, its superior acoustics have ushered in a new and more promising era for classical music.

As far as concertgoers in New York are concerned, the favorite composer of opera is the German, Wolfgang Amadeus Mozart. The very first opera performed here was his *Don Giovanni* and it remains a favorite although *The Magic Flute* is even more popular. Many of Mozart's other works are featured each year, especially his violin and piano

Actors perform a scene from John Gay's Beggar's Opera. *New York's stage performances are quite popular, and it is important to arrive at the theater early enough to purchase a ticket.*

concertos because of the popularity of these two instruments.

New York does not yet have a full orchestra, and because of this temporary shortcoming, music lovers must be content to hear small baroque orchestras of twenty to twenty-five musicians. Music lovers are feverishly working to double and triple the size of the orchestra because of a twenty-three-year-old talented and promising German composer by the

name of Ludwig van Beethoven who writes for full orchestra and piano. This would be especially exciting because in 1770 New York received its first piano, and since that time pianos have been slowly replacing all harpsichords.

Even the smaller orchestras play many compositions by Baroque German and Italian composers such as Corelli, Vivaldi, and Handel. Christmas is the favorite time for music when Handel's

Messiah is performed. The audience is encouraged to join in with the singing of the *Hallelujah Chorus*.

Tickets to each season's offerings are sold as a set. Depending upon the number of offerings and the location of the seats, season tickets cost between five and seven dollars. Visitors, who are not likely to hold season tickets, may purchase them the day of performances from ticket holders not able to attend.

Private Clubs

New York also has a small number of elite private social clubs. Available to only well-heeled New Yorkers, many wealthy families are no longer willing to entertain in the city's finer public taverns because of the lack of privacy. For many refined New Yorkers interested in entertaining family, friends, and business associates in a grand sophisticated style, these private clubs are the places to do it.

Another attraction of private social clubs is their convenience. Socially prominent families have learned that elegant dinner parties are expensive and exhausting. Families interested in social whirls found themselves spending more money on parties than any other activity and hiring more help than ever. Prominent dinner parties required hiring reliable cooks and servers while additional slaves were needed to stable horses and carriages, provide wood for cooking and heating, and cleaning the entire house before dinner guests arrived and again after they had departed. In the long run, joining one of the city's social clubs, if an invitation is offered, turns out to be the best solution.

The organ loft at Trinity Church is decorated with elaborately hand-carved woodwork.

Colonial New York

Private social clubs have heightened the emphasis in New York on social prestige and class consciousness. If visitors wish to experience New York's high society, an invitation from a member is required. Some of the most highly prized invitations are from the City Assembly, the Juvenile Assembly, and the Friendly Club; however, the most exclusive and most difficult to experience is an evening at the Belvedere House that just recently opened last year.

The Belvedere House is located between Cherry and Montgomery Streets. Its architectural style is in keeping with many new Federalist homes featuring a large grand entry porch for carriages with four massive white columns supporting the roof. Inside, the Belvedere House offers members for their enjoyment an elegant octagonal ballroom, two private dining parlors, two card rooms, a barroom, and overnight accommodations for

New York's Newspapers

Newspapers have been a fixture of the city's political and intellectual life for almost seventy years. As a source of news, they have kept New Yorkers up-to-date on both foreign and domestic issues. As a source of advertising, they have served to notify the public about sales of goods and land. As a source of commerce, they announce the arrival and departure of all ships. As a source of culture, they notify the public about theater, music, and museum openings. Without them, New York would not be able to make the claim of being the most cosmopolitan city in America.

New York's first newspaper, the *New York Gazette,* published the city's first issue almost seventy years ago on November 8, 1725. The *Gazette* continues to be printed at its original site on Hanover Street. Initially the *Gazette* was a small, rather poorly printed two-page newspaper that was distributed and sold on a weekly basis. It contained mostly news that was sometimes several months old by the time it got to the printing press. Typically the two pages included news from England, legal announcements, a list of

ships that had entered and departed the port, and a few advertisements. In 1725 a young man from Boston, Benjamin Franklin, applied for a position with the newspaper but was turned down because there were no available positions. Fortunately for America, Franklin found work elsewhere.

When friction began to develop between patriotic New Yorkers and the English, many felt that the *Gazette* was far too loyal to the Crown. This sentiment motivated John Holt to start the second newspaper in the city in 1766, the *New York Weekly Journal.* Holt was a patriot and supported the cause of the American Revolution. Holt and his newspaper maintained their stance for liberty and because of their anti-English editorial comments, were forced to evacuate the city in 1776 when the British occupied it.

All newspapers began as small two-page papers that eventually expanded to the current eight-page papers that are folded in half and sold on the streets. It is the tradition in New York to purchase a paper, read it, and then pass it on to other readers at no charge.

The Belvedere House provides accommodations, fine dining, and entertainment. The club also houses a fine collection of art, including a painting of Venice by Canaletto.

a few members. One of the more unusual and attractive features of the Belvedere House is its collection of fine art bought from galleries in England, France, and Italy. The most revered paintings are a garden scene by the French painter Antoine Watteau and a painting of a canal in Venice, Italy, by Giovanni Antonio Canal who more commonly goes by the name Canaletto.

Chapter 8

Quality Shopping in New York

N ew York has the greatest shopping. No other major city can match the variety and quality of goods found here. As New Yorkers recover from the destruction of the war and as the economy returns to normal, shopping opportunities abound.

Nothing is quite like shopping on lower Broadway around the Bowling Green in ward number one. This is the neighborhood of the wealthiest New Yorkers who demand the finest clothing, interior decorations, and personal items. The boutiques in this area are elegant and the shop keepers polite to all customers. Other great shops can also be found along the docks. Queen Street, for example, is a festival of America's swashbuckling maritime spirit with nautical shops facing the tall sailing ships and the activity of a thriving seaport. And for bargain hunters, in the far north end of Nassau Street is a place where visitors on a budget can find merchants willing to

Broadway's shops sell quality goods such as the elegant clothing this gentleman is wearing.

The Empress of China

One of the most extraordinary events to occur annually in New York is the arrival of the ship *Empress of China* that makes regularly scheduled trips between New York and Canton, China. When it docks, young boys and girls flood the wharf to see it come in and New York shoppers know that within a day or two many shops will be filled with exotic wares of all sorts from the mystical East.

The distance that the ship travels, halfway around the world, means that it is capable of only one round-trip per year. It departs New York in February, arrives in Canton in August, and is back in New York in February the following year. This great oceangoing vessel provides merchants with a wide variety of exotic commodities found nowhere else, such as silk and satin clothing, hand-painted wallpaper, lacquered fans, umbrellas, exotic dried plants used as medicines, porcelain dinnerware called "china" because of where it is made, and even the delectable Shanghai roosters that arrive alive, ready to be sold to New York's finest taverns for their well-heeled clientele.

Of all the products from China, porcelain remains the favorite. The brilliant blue and white wares, some of them two hundred years old dating back to the Ming dynasty, are preferred by wealthy families that can afford one or two large bowls. A few New York families have even managed to collect entire servings of the porcelain found nowhere else in America. This is the same famous porcelain that the English, French, Spanish, and Dutch have been collecting for several generations.

The *Empress of China* draws a crowd when it sails into the harbor not only because of its merchandise and destination, but also because of its copper bottom and black painted hull, all of which lend great mystery to her presence. If luck is with you, and she is in port during your visit, walk down to Whitehall Slip at the foot of the Battery to see the vessel.

haggle over a curious assortment of odds and ends.

Some of the best small specialty shops can be found on public grounds. On the skirts of the large open grassy field called the New York Common, small businesses open in temporary tent shops that must be removed nightly. This is one spot in the city for shoppers to find goods produced exclusively by local artisans such as watchmakers, furniture makers, portrait artists, pewterers and potters, silversmiths, perfumers, glovers, and seamstresses.

Other craftsmen who offer services rather than goods also set up shops along many smaller streets. They offer their services as chimney sweeps, bootblacks, knife sharpeners, furniture repairmen, and rag and bottle pickers. Some of these merchants use distinctive signs that hang from their shop doors advertising their craft. Barbers, for example, set out a striped red and white pole, locksmiths display cutouts of oversize keys, gunsmiths hang enlarged wooden pistols from their doors, pawnshop dealers hang three gold-colored balls from their front doors, and apothecaries display an enlarged mortar and pestle.

Of the many goods available in New York, a few are more unusual than others and also more difficult to find outside a big city such as ours. While you are here, why not take advantage of the opportunity to stock up on things such as quills and ink, take care of printing needs, purchase a fancy new saddle, and look for colorful glass gifts to take home for friends and relatives.

Quills and Ink

New York is arguably the best place to replenish your writing supplies. Several stationery shops exist in the city. The market for quills is strong albeit a small market. Merchants as well as literate New Yorkers need to write letters, record business receipts, fill out documents for trade, and record all of the city's legal actions.

No two quills write the same because each shaft is unique and because each is trimmed differently by the quill maker.

New York's merchants offer some of the country's finest writing supplies. Customers are invited to try out handmade quills and colorful inks before purchasing.

The Art of the Quill

Selecting a good quill requires experience and care. The best and strongest quills are those taken from living birds during the spring when they have just molted and replaced all of their feathers. Of the feathers, the very finest are the five outer feathers of the left wing. The left wing is favored because the feathers curve outward and away when used by a right-handed writer, which includes just about everyone. The feathers that hold their tip the longest are those from the swan and for this reason, they are the most expensive. They also have the unique ability to hold ink in the feather shaft until light pressure is applied, allowing the ink to flow. After swan feathers, goose feathers are preferred, followed by the less expensive crow, eagle, owl, hawk, and finally turkey feathers. It is commonly known that geese are specially bred by Thomas Jefferson to supply his own vast need for quills.

When purchasing a good quality quill pen, the tip will be precisely cut at an angle and then split down the middle with a very small knife appropriately called a pen knife. The angle of the cut determines the thickness of the line. Since the tip gradually spreads the more it is dipped into ink, pay attention to the angle so when you return home, you will be able to trim the tip at the same angle. A good quill holds enough ink after dipping it into an inkwell to write three to five words. If used regularly, tips wear away quickly from pressure and from trimming to last no more than one full day.

Discriminating customers purchase fine quills like this one that is part of an elegant writing set made of silver.

Therefore, the shopkeeper allows a customer to try out his quills to get a feel for how they write. The careful selection, cleaning, trimming, and delicate sanding of each quill are tedious jobs requiring a skilled quill maker.

Inks come in many colors and are sold as dry powder by the gram or by the ounce. Most common is black made from finely crushed black carbon called lampblack. Other inks of various colors, although very expensive and rarely used, are made from fungi that grow on oak and nut trees or berries, pulverized minerals, crushed insects, and a variety of shellfish.

Printing a Broadside

Printers who played a significant role in the Revolution are available to print any sort of book or broadside. Most acquired their skills in the months leading up to the war by printing thousands of broadsides and pamphlets denouncing the English while extolling democracy. In addition, New York printers also print advertisements, business forms, laws and proclamations, customized record books, and even the paper currency.

The cost for a printing job should be the first consideration. Cost is determined by the number of sheets, size of sheets, quality of paper, and the number of letters in the job. Once a price and layout are agreed upon, the printer gets to work. Because of the possibility for error, printers prefer that customers stay at the shop or be available when called to proofread and select paper from the available stock.

New York printers prefer to use iron type imported from the Netherlands. A workman called the compositor sets each letter in each printed line into an iron rule, called a composing stick, used to lock words into straight, evenly spaced lines. Each letter must be set backward because

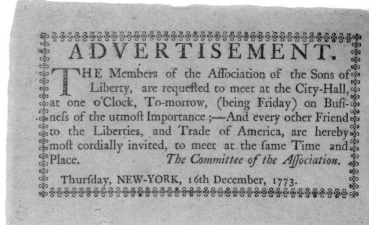

The Sons of Liberty distributed locally printed broadsides like this on the streets of New York.

printing reverses the image. When several lines are set, the compositor locks them in wooden cases called galleys. One sheet of small print, such as a newspaper, takes an experienced compositor about twenty-four hours to complete. Once all letters are set, a proof is pressed and checked for spelling errors. It is recommended that the person paying for the print job be available to double-check for spelling errors because this is the last opportunity to do so without incurring additional cost.

When the call to "roll the press" is called out, the pressman carries the galleys over to the press where the printing is performed. The galleys are tied with string, gathered and locked in a page-size iron frame, or chase, and secured to the stone bed of the press. At this time, the customer may again be asked to approve the paper before the galleys are inked for printing. Paper stocks are highly unpredictable because paper is difficult to acquire and available choices can change from day to day.

The beater, the helper who applies the ink, uses two wood-handled leather-covered ink rollers stuffed with cotton to roll lampblack ink evenly over the type. The presser lays a single sheet of slightly moistened paper into a frame and cranks up the chase until it squeezes against the paper, making the ink impression. The sheet is then pulled off and set aside to dry.

Saddles

These days everyone needs a good saddle. The city is choked with horses, nearly all of which are in need of saddles and bridles. New York has harness makers capable of crafting saddles to accommodate everyone's personal needs and budget. A saddle is one product that is both practical and stylish. The choice of style and quality of leather reflect a person's profession and social standing in the community. Since you have come to a sophisticated city, why not visit one of the city's finest harness makers for a fine custom work of art?

Hammermeyer's Harness Works is such a place. Located out along the palisades at the intersection of Queen and Banker Streets, Mr. Hammermeyer is the man to ask for. When selecting a saddle, Hammermeyer will ask you to bring your horse so the saddle can be custom fitted to its back. The less expensive ready-made saddles rarely fit properly and many horses seen on the street suffer under the weight of their riders for this reason. He will also ask your budget range because an ordinary saddle costs roughly a month's wages for a professional man but three times that for the highest quality leather and detailed craftsmanship.

Handcrafted leather saddles come in a variety of styles.

Purchasing Snuff

New York has experienced a recent rash of wealthy citizens sniffing snuff, a pulverized form of tobacco mixed with a variety of exotic spices and herbs, up their noses. The sniffing act is quickly followed by an explosion of sneezes expelling the snuff into the gentleman's handkerchief. Although most New Yorkers frown on this somewhat silly and disgusting habit, those who use this substance claim that it clears the sinuses while curing a variety of ailments.

Snuff can be purchased at tobacco shops in ward number one along Broadway. Shopkeepers sell it along with other tobacco products. Snuff is normally purchased by the ounce and it can be had in a variety of "flavors" depending upon the type of herbs mixed into the powdered tobacco. Small quantities are sold in tiny glass bowls while large quantities are packaged in animal bladders that are cleaned and tanned before being filled.

Some men purchase snuff because of a belief that it has health benefits. According to Elizabeth Wyckoff in her article "The Sneezing Cure," the French writer Louis Ferrant claims that snuff provides, "An excellent cephalic purge to those who love their health . . . and the humors purged by snuff do not affect the seat of reason."

A gentleman takes snuff, a popular habit among New Yorkers. Visitors can purchase snuff and related items at tobacco shops along Broadway.

After the horse has been measured, Hammermeyer instructs an apprentice to make a wood frame that will later be covered by the leather. The frame is called a "tree" and careful carving and gluing will guarantee a comfortable saddle as well as a long-lasting one; twenty-five to thirty years of use can be expected from a well-assembled saddle. Prior to the application of leather, the tree is inspected on the horse for proper fit.

Next the leather is selected. This is the most expensive part of the saddle. The highest quality grain is calfskin that has no scars from injuries, fence cuts, or other puncture wounds. Lower quality scarred leather is also available. Following leather selection, the wood tree is covered; then the low backrest, called the cantle, and the seat, the panels that protect the horse from the riders legs, and finally the stirrups, are stitched and attached. Total weight is generally between twenty and twenty-five pounds.

Decorative leather carvings are an optional final touch. Some gentlemen want their monogram carved on one side, others fancy floral designs, and still others their family's crest. Start to finish, expect the job to take between four and seven days.

Glass

Glass remains one of the most difficult household commodities to find in New York. This is true throughout America as well because the process is difficult to learn and factories are difficult and ex-pensive to build. For these reasons, most glass made in New York is used for practical applications such as windowpanes, bottles, and glass display cases for retail stores. One of the great advantages of being in New York, however, is the availability of a few high-end expensive shops that cater to the upper class. These shops carry an array of fine long-stemmed wine goblets, wine decanters, water pitchers, perfume bottles, and flower vases.

Some of these glass products can be purchased at affordable prices when the glassmaker uses iron molds to shape them. This rather new innovation, first developed in Amsterdam, allows the glassmaker to pour the very hot liquefied glass into a hinged form until it hardens, at which time the form is opened and the product removed. These types of glass containers are popular but they have the drawback of all being exactly alike with a noticeable seam where the two halves of the mold clamped together.

Custom glass products, on the other hand, are unique but pricey. Even simple glass items such as butter plates and candlestick holders are not cheap, and prices climb if colored glass is desired and climb again if decorative cutting is requested. Although many buyers prefer the clear crystal look of decorative glass, recent innovations adding color have also become popular. Most of New York's glass shops now offer a variety of green shades for bottles, maroon paper weights, amethyst sugar bowls, and cobalt blue water pitchers.

Colonial New York

The proprietors of a few shops may allow you to watch the glassmaking process in the back work area. There you can see and feel the intense heat of the small brick oven called the "crucible." It melts glass at extremely high temperatures into a white-hot molten mass before it is shaped. When the viscosity is just right, the "gaffer," the man who blows air into the hot liquid mass to shape it, removes a glob on the end of a long pipe. As he blows into the wood-covered cool end of the pipe, the glob inflates into a bubble. Using a variety of tools, the blown glob is shaped and cooled.

A glassblower twirls molten glass in the kiln's white-hot flame. Watching the process is as entertaining as shopping for the finished product.

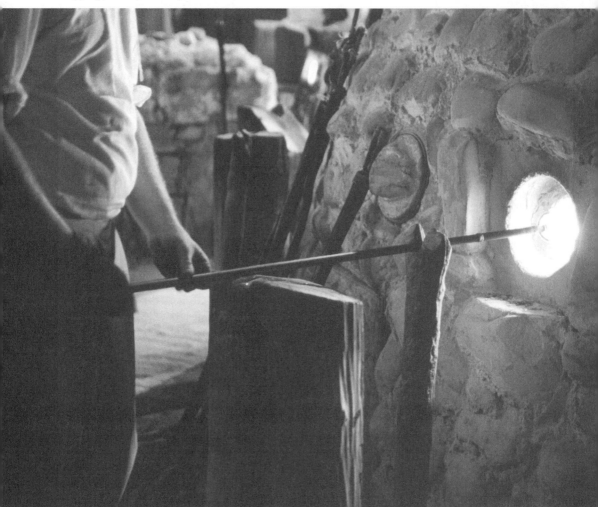

If decorative cutting is requested, the cooled finished product is incised with very hard grinding wheels. The art is to cut designs into the surface of the glass but not to cut through the glass. When completed, cut colored glass placed in the sunlight sparkles. There is no doubt that New York glassmakers rival their British counterparts in England.

These elegant goblets are only a sample of the fine glassware available for purchase as gifts and souvenirs.

A day stocking up on gifts for friends and family may be a fitting way to end a vacation in New York. Much like the city itself, the shops are distinctive, stylish, of high quality, and gladly purvey to all classes of New Yorkers.

Notes

Chapter One: A Brief History

1. Quoted in Samuel Eliot Morison: *The European Discovery of America: The Northern Voyages* A.D. 500–1600. New York: Oxford University Press, 1971, p. 23.
2. Quoted in Edwin G. Burrows and Mike Wallace, *Gotham: A History of New York City to 1898.* New York: Oxford University Press, 1999, p. xiv.
3. Quoted in Kenneth T. Jackson, *The Encyclopedia of New York City.* New Haven, CT: Yale University Press, 1995, p. 199.
4. Quoted in Jackson, *The Encyclopedia of New York City,* p. 203.
5. Quoted in Burrows and Wallace, *Gotham,* p. 267.
6. Quoted in Burrows and Wallace, *Gotham,* p. 267.
7. Quoted in Burrows and Wallace, *Gotham,* p. 283.

Chapter Two: Arriving, Location, and Weather

8. Quoted in Jackson, *The Encyclopedia of New York City,* p. 408.

Chapter Three: First Day: Getting Around and Where to Eat

9. Quoted in Burrows and Wallace, *Gotham,* p. 338.

Chapter Four: Five Historic Landmarks

10. Quoted in New Netherland Project, "New Amsterdam," 2002. www.nnp.org.
11. Quoted in New Netherland Project, "New Amsterdam," 2002.
12. Quoted in Burrows and Wallace, *Gotham,* p. 176.
13. Columbia University, "A Brief History of Columbia," 1999. www.columbia.edu.

Chapter Five: Island Tours

14. Quoted in Sharon Seitz and Stuart Miller, *The Other Islands of New York: A Historical Companion.* Woodstock, VT: Countryman, 1996, p. 57.

Chapter Six: Casual Entertainment

15. Quoted in Jackson, *The Encyclopedia of New York City,* p. 694.
16. Quoted in Paul Moran, "Belmont Horse Racing," Newsday.com, 2002. www.newsday.com.
17. Quoted in Robert Baldick, *The Duel: A History of Duelling.* London: Chapman and Hall, 1965, p. 28.

Chapter Seven: Cultural New York

18. Quoted in Burrows and Wallace, *Gotham,* p. 374.
19. Quoted in Susan Elizabeth Lyman, *The Story of New York: An Informal History of the City.* New York: Crown, 1964, p. 101.

For Further Reading

Michael J. Anuta, *Ships of Our Ancestors*. New York: Genealogical, 1999. The author provides an extensive list of sailing ships, their histories, and photographs documenting immigration from Europe to America during the eighteenth and nineteenth centuries.

Sylvia G.L. Dannett, *The Yankee Doodler*. New York: A.S. Barnes, 1973. This book provides a collection of political cartoons published in New York newspapers during the colonial period. They reflect American hatred of the English and their repressive economic and political policies.

Eric Homberger, *The Historical Atlas of New York City: A Visual Celebration of Nearly 400 Years of New York City's History*. New York: Henry Holt, 1998. The author of this book provides an excellent overview of New York City's history from the arrival of the Dutch to the present era. One of the book's great strengths is its collection of maps and photographs.

Thomas Janvier, *In Old New York: A Classic History of New York City*. New York: St. Martin's, 2000. This book presents a fascinating history of New York from the arrival of the Dutch through the eighteenth century. Filled with interesting anecdotal information, entries from memoirs, maps, and hand-drawn sketches of places and streets, the book brings early New York back to life.

William Kornblum, *At Sea in the City: New York from the Water's Edge*. Chapel Hill, NC: Algonquin, 2002. Kornblum provides an entertaining history of the harbor of New York City that includes several chapters describing the harbor, its many islands, and ships of the colonial period.

New York City Landmarks Preservation Commission, *Guide to New York City Landmarks*. New York: John Wiley & Sons, 1998. This book is essentially a travel guide to the historical landmarks of the city. It includes a good selection of sites, principally in Lower Manhattan, many of which date back to the colonial and precolonial periods.

Works Consulted

Books

Robert Baldick, *The Duel: A History of Duelling.* London: Chapman and Hall, 1965. Everything imaginable about the art and history of dueling can be found in this book. The author provides a comprehensive account of all manner of dueling although most of the book addresses the use, rules, and lore of swords and pistols.

Edwin G. Burrows and Mike Wallace, *Gotham: A History of New York City to 1898.* New York: Oxford University Press, 1999. This Pulitzer Prize–winning book is a twelve-hundred-page compendium filled with thousands of interesting bits of information that collectively paint a comprehensive portrait of this remarkable city.

Anne-Marie Cantwell and Dianna di Zerega Wall, *Unearthing Gotham: The Archaeology of New York City.* New Haven, CT: Yale University Press, 2001. As the name suggests, this book catalogs many of the interesting discoveries of colonial New York unearthed by contemporary archaeologists. Based on the artifacts discovered, historians have been able to provide a more thorough history of the city.

Kenneth T. Jackson, *The Encyclopedia of New York City.* New Haven, CT: Yale University Press, 1995. This is an encyclopedia, from A to Z, that contains thousands of short entries documenting the history of well-known New York people, places, societies, monuments, and institutions.

Michael G. Kammen, *Colonial New York: A History.* White Plains, NY: KTO, 1987. This book includes the political, social, economic, cultural, and religious aspects of New York's early years from the city's founding through the Revolutionary

War. Kammen presents life in colonial New York as a precursor to contemporary American society and culture.

Susan Elizabeth Lyman, *The Story of New York: An Informal History of the City*. New York: Crown, 1964. The author provides an excellent short history of New York City. The chapters that address the colonial period are amply represented and the old maps and hand-drawn pictures are helpful for gaining an understanding of the early years of the city.

Samuel Eliot Morison, *The European Discovery of America: The Northern Voyages* A.D. *500–1600*. New York: Oxford University Press, 1971. The author provides a comprehensive account of all the known voyages by Europeans to the New World from the sixth through the seventeenth centuries. Morison tells compelling stories about the explorers who made dangerous journeys and the impact of their discoveries after they returned to Europe to report them.

Sharon Seitz and Stuart Miller, *The Other Islands of New York: A Historical Companion*. Woodstock, VT: Countryman, 1996. The authors of this guide to the lesser-known islands of New York have picked twenty small islands to describe. Each island is introduced with its places of interest, things to do, the island's history, and information about places to eat and stay.

Norval White, *New York: A Physical History*. New York: Atheneum, 1987. The first four chapters of this book address the early periods of New York's architectural heritage. In addition to excellent textual descriptions of significant early buildings, the author provides original drawings and maps.

Internet Sources

Ian Chadwick, "Henry Hudson," Ian Chadwick's Web Sites, 2000. www.ianchadwick.com.

Columbia University, "A Brief History of Columbia," 1999. www.columbia.edu.

John T. Humphrey, "Traveling to America," Genealogy, 2003. www.genealogy.about.com.

Lee Lawrence, "Chronicling Black Lives in Colonial New England," *Christian Science Monitor*, 2003. www.csmweb2.emcweb.com.

The Learning Channel, "Independence at Bowling Green," 2000. http://tlc.discovery.com.

Benson J. Lossing, "George Washington 1st President." www.publicbookshelf.com.

Paul Moran, "Belmont Horse Racing," Newsday.com, 2002. www.newsday.com.

Napoleon Bonaparte Internet Guide, "New York Ordinaries," 1997. www.napoleonbonaparte.nl.

New Jersey Lighthouse Society, "Sandy Hook Lighthouse," 1999. www.njlhs.burlco.org.

New Netherland Project, "New Amsterdam," 2002. www.nnp.org.

Public Broadcasting System, "The Dutch West Indies Company," 2002. www.pbs.org.

Elizabeth Wyckoff, "The Sneezing Cure," New York Public Library, 1997. www.nypl.org.

Index

Picture Credits

Cover image: © Francis G. Mayer/CORBIS
The American Revolution: A Picture Sourcebook, Dover Publications, Inc., 9, 21, 43, 44
© James L. Amos/CORBIS, 98
Animals, Dover Publications, Inc., 70, 71
© Archivo Iconografico, S.A./CORBIS, 72 (bottom), 79
© Bettmann/CORBIS, 38, 56, 83
© Burstein Collection/CORBIS, 86
© Geoffrey Clements/CORBIS, 90
© CORBIS, 12, 32, 64, 87
Corel, 7, 89
Dictionary of American Portraits, Dover Publications, Inc., 63
Food and Drink, Dover Publications, Inc., 39, 45, 46
Harter's Picture Archive, Dover Publications, Inc., 25
Hulton/Archive by Getty Images, 42, 51, 52, 55, 74, 95
© Richard I'Anson/Lonely Planet Images, 36
Joseph Paris Picture Archives, 6, 10, 15 (bottom), 17, 18–19, 37, 48
© Danny Lehman/CORBIS, 47
Library of Congress, 72 (top), 78, 94
© David Muench/CORBIS, 68
© Museum of the City of New York/CORBIS, 62, 67, 82
Music, Dover Publications, Inc., 85
Brandy Noon, 50, 61
© North Wind Picture Archives, 8, 11 (both), 13, 14, 20, 23, 26–27, 29, 41, 49, 59, 60, 76
© Richard T. Nowitz/CORBIS, 92, 96
Pictorial Archive of Early Illustrations and Views of American Architecture, Dover Publications, Inc., 57, 65
Picture History, 75
© Stapleton Collection/CORBIS, 35
© Stock Montage, Inc., 15 (top), 16, 31, 33, 54
Trades and Occupations, Dover Publications, Inc., 34, 66, 81
© Adam Woolfitt/CORBIS, 93
© Tim Wright/CORBIS, 99
Courtesy of the Wyckoff House & Association, 69

About the Author

James Barter received his undergraduate degree in history and classics at the University of California at Berkeley followed by graduate studies in ancient history and archaeology at the University of Pennsylvania. Mr. Barter has taught history as well as Latin and Greek.

A Fulbright scholar at the American Academy in Rome, Mr. Barter worked on archaeological sites in and around the city as well as on sites in the Naples area. He also has worked and traveled extensively in Greece.

Mr. Barter currently lives in Rancho Santa Fe, California.